Scale Construction and Psychometrics for Social and Personality Psychology

The SAGE Library of Methods in Social and Personality Psychology is a new series of books to provide students and researchers in these fields with an understanding of the methods and techniques essential to conducting cutting-edge research.

Each volume explains a specific topic and has been written by an active scholar (or scholars) with expertise in that particular methodological domain. Assuming no prior knowledge of the topic, the volumes are clear and accessible for all readers. In each volume, a topic is introduced, applications are discussed, and readers are led step by step through worked examples. In addition, advice about how to interpret and prepare results for publication is presented.

The Library should be particularly valuable for advanced students and academics who want to know more about how to use research methods and who want experience-based advice from leading scholars in social and personality psychology.

Published titles:
Jim Blascovich, Eric J. Vanman, Wendy Berry Mendes, Sally Dickerson, *Social Psychophysiology for Social and Personality Psychology*

R. Michael Furr, *Scale Construction and Psychometrics for Social and Personality Psychology*

Rick H. Hoyle, *Structural Equation Modeling for Social and Personality Psychology*

John B. Nezlek, *Multilevel Modeling for Social and Personality Psychology*

Laurie A. Rudman, *Implicit Measures for Social and Personality Psychology*

Forthcoming titles:
John B. Nezlek, *Diary Methods for Social and Personality Psychology*

The SAGE Library of Methods in Social and Personality Psychology

Scale Construction and Psychometrics for Social and Personality Psychology

R. Michael Furr

Los Angeles | London | New Delhi
Singapore | Washington DC

First Published 2011

SAGE Publications Ltd
1 Oliver's Yard
55 City Road
London EC1Y 1SP

SAGE Publications Inc.
2455 Teller Road
Thousand Oaks, California 91320

SAGE Publications India Pvt Ltd
B 1/I 1 Mohan Cooperative Industrial Area
Mathura Road
New Delhi 110 044

SAGE Publications Asia-Pacific Pte Ltd
33 Pekin Street #02–01
Far East Square
Singapore 048763

Library of Congress Control Number: 2010935088

British Library Cataloguing in Publication data

A catalogue record for this book is available from the British Library

ISBN 978-0-85702-404-6

Typeset by C&M Digitals (P) Ltd, Chennai, India
Printed by MPG Books Group, Bodmin, Cornwall
Printed on paper from sustainable resources

Contents

1

Introduction

Social and personality psychologists often use psychological inventories, tests, or questionnaires to measure important psychological phenomena. Indeed, such instruments may be the most widely-used method of measuring variables such as attitudes, traits, self-concept, self-evaluation, beliefs, abilities, motivation, goals, social perceptions, and so on. In both experimental and non-experimental research, social and personality psychologists often rely upon previously-developed scales, develop entirely new scales, or generate revised scales based upon those developed by other researchers when measuring one or more variables. These methods have produced important advances, revealing the psychological mechanisms underlying many important psychological phenomena.

The current volume provides a conceptual and practical foundation for producers and consumers of research based upon psychological scales. More specifically, it addresses issues in scale construction, scale use, scale evaluation, and interpretation of research results emerging from psychological scales. It covers basic principles, practices, and processes, and it introduces advanced techniques that expand one's psychometric toolkit. In covering these issues, the volume highlights their fundamental importance for the analysis and interpretation of psychological research, and it provides relatively non-technical discussions intended to facilitate basic appreciation, understanding, and interest.

Attention to psychometrics and measurement seems somewhat compartmentalized. Some, perhaps many, researchers view psychometrics and measurement as relevant only for the study of "individual differences," for "correlational research," and/or for self-report scales.

Such perceptions are incorrect. In fact, psychometrics and measurement are important for all psychological research—experimental and non-experimental research, research-based self-reports and research based upon behavioral observations, physiological data, reaction times, and other form of measurement used in social/personality psychology. Regardless of the internal validity of one's research, the importance of one's research questions, or the apparent objectivity of one's measurement strategy, psychometric issues such as dimensionality, reliability, and validity have important implications for one's ability to draw meaningful conclusions from psychological research.

Importance of Well-grounded Scale Construction and Psychometric Understanding

Effective scale construction and adequate psychometric quality have important implications for the proper interpretation of psychological research and its psychological meaning. An important goal of this volume is to articulate several such implications—hopefully providing broader insight into the importance of strong measurement.

First, the quality of our measures affects the apparent size of effects obtained in our analyses. According to basic psychometric theory, the apparent association between any two variables is affected directly by the reliability of the measures of one or more of those variables. More specifically, imperfect reliability reduces, or attenuates, the effects actually observed in one's research, as compared with the true psychological effects. This is true for experimental research as much as for non-experimental research. Whether a particular analysis involves manipulated independent variables and measured dependent variables or it involves several measured variables, the reliability of the measured variables directly affects the resulting magnitude of the differences or associations.

Second, by affecting the sizes of statistical effects, measurement quality indirectly affects the statistical significance of those effects. Of course, the size of an observed difference or the size of an observed correlation directly affects the likelihood that the difference or correlation will reach statistical significance. Thus, if poor measurement quality produces an attenuated effect for a given group difference, main effect, interaction effect, correlation, or regression slope, then that effect is relatively unlikely to reach statistical significance.

Third, the quality of one's measures (and manipulations) affects the psychological meaning of one's results. That is, the psychological meaning of a scale's scores has important implications for the psychological inferences to be drawn from research using that scale. If the scores have clear meaning in terms of a psychological construct, then any research using the scale can be interpreted confidently with regard to that construct. However, if a scale's scores have ambiguous or undemonstrated psychological meaning, then research using the scale cannot be interpreted confidently in terms of any particular psychological construct. More generally, if a measurement process lacks empirically-demonstrated validity evidence, then researchers cannot draw well-grounded inferences about its psychological implications. However, if a measurement process is constructed with attention to psychometric quality, then researchers—both producers and consumers of the research—can confidently interpret the size and statistical significance of the result, and they can make well-grounded psychological inferences.

This volume will examine these implications in depth, reviewing procedures that are valuable for producers and consumers of psychological research. For producers, this volume hopefully enhances motivation and ability to implement effective and well-understood measurement strategies. For producers and consumers of psychological research, it hopefully enhances motivation and ability to interpret research within the proper psychometric context—understanding the implications of specific measurement strategies, understanding how to evaluate the quality of those strategies, and understanding the ways in which measurement quality affects psychological conclusions.

Overview

After briefly highlighting basic principles, practices, and recommendations, this volume provides guidance and background helping social/personality psychologists construct, use, evaluate, and interpret psychological measures. The first section describes steps in the construction of psychometrically-sound scales, it introduces basic psychometric properties such as dimensionality, reliability, and validity, and it examines potential threats to psychometric quality. The second section introduces special topics and advanced psychometric perspectives, focussing on the use of difference scores, and on the logic and use of Confirmatory Factor Analysis, Generalizability Theory, and Item Response Theory as advanced psychometric perspectives. These advanced perspectives differ in important ways from the traditional psychometric perspective with which most readers might be familiar.

2

Core Principles, Best Practices, and an Overview of Scale Construction

This chapter presents principles and practices that are among the broadest and most fundamental issues for scale construction, modification, use, evaluation, and interpretation. The points are rather straightforward but are vitally important in conducting informative research. Thus, this chapter provides nontechnical overviews of each point, to be complemented by greater exploration and depth later in this volume.

Several of these principles and practices strike me, as an editor, reviewer, and reader of social/personality research, as being somewhat under-appreciated. To retain focus on those issues, this chapter bypasses issues that, though fundamental to scale construction and psychometrics, seem generally well-known and well-implemented. Indeed, much social/personality research is based upon measurement that is well-conceived and appropriately-executed. This discussion is intended to raise awareness and understanding of issues that, if appreciated even more widely, will enhance the generally good conduct and interpretation of research. The issues are summarized in Table 2.1.

Most facets of the process and principles covered in this chapter apply to all forms of psychological measurement. For example, this chapter addresses the need to articulate the construct and context of a measurement strategy, the need to evaluate psychometric properties, and the need to revise the measurement strategy if necessary—all of which apply to measurement strategies such as "tests" of maximal performance, reaction time, behavioral observations, physiological, measures, choices and decisions, informant-reports, and so on.

In addition, this chapter outlines scale construction in terms of four steps (Figure 2.1). Reflecting contemporary social/personality psychology (John & Benet-Martinez, 2000), this chapter (and this volume more generally) blends several approaches to scale construction. It involves rationally-focussed item-writing, attention to scale dimensionality and internal coherence, and empirical examination of the scale's psychological meaning.

Table 2.1   Under-appreciated principles and practices in scale construction, use, evaluation, and interpretation

Principles and practices

1   Examination and interpretation of reliability and validity
   a)   Psychometric properties and quality *of the current data* should be evaluated
   b)   Psychometric properties and quality *of the current data* should be considered when using scales and when drawing psychological implications from observed effects

2   Dimensionality (i.e., factor structure)
   a)   Dimensionality should be evaluated and considered in scale construction, use, and evaluation
   b)   Coefficient alpha is not an index of unidimensionality, the "eigenvalue greater than one" rule should be avoided, and oblique rotations are preferable to orthogonal rotations

3   Ad hoc scales
   a)   Previously-validated scales are preferable to ad hoc scales
   b)   Ad hoc scales should be examined psychometrically, requiring more than assumed face validity

4   Modified scales
   a)   Previously-validated original scales are preferable to modified scales
   b)   Modified scales should be examined psychometrically, not assumed to have the same dimensionality, reliability, and validity of original scales

5   Brief/single-item scales
   a)   Sufficiently-long scales are preferable to overly-brief scales
   b)   Brief/single-item scales should be examined psychometrically, and their psychometric quality and potential limitations should be appropriately discussed

6   The use of scales across groups
   a)   If scales are used in groups that might differ psychologically from those within which the scales were developed and validated, then the psychometric properties/differences should be examined, understood, and potentially rectified
   b)   Careful translation does not guarantee psychometric stability across linguistically-differing groups

7   Difference scores (i.e., gain scores, change scores, discrepancy scores)
   a)   Alternatives to difference scores should be considered strongly
   b)   Difference scores should be used only with attention to their components and their psychometric quality

8   Advanced psychometric perspectives (e.g., Confirmatory Factor Analysis, Generalizability Theory, and Item Response Theory)
   a)   Advanced perspectives offer some important differences/advantages, as compared to traditional psychometric theory; thus, they might be highly-appropriate methods of understanding and evaluating the psychometric properties of a given scale
   b)   Producers and consumers of research should be prepared to provide and/or interpret information obtained from these perspectives when necessary

Examination and Interpretation of Reliability and Validity

First and most broadly, the psychometric quality *of the current data* should be evaluated and considered when interpreting results. Reliability and validity are

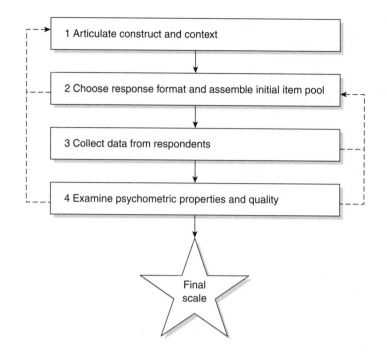

Figure 2.1 The scale construction process

crucial in understanding statistical results and their psychological implications. Roughly stated, reliability is the precision of scores—the degree to which scores accurately reflect some psychological variable in a given sample. Validity, then, concerns the "some variable" reflected by those scores—specifically, validity is the degree to which scores can be interpreted in terms of a specific psychological construct. Note that scores can be reliable (i.e., they can be good indicators of something), but—at the same time—they can be interpreted invalidly (i.e., they can be interpreted in terms of a construct that they do not truly reflect).

Thus, there are at least two issues that should be addressed in any psychological study. The first is the psychometric properties and qualities of the measures used in the study. Reliability and validity are fundamental facets of psychometric quality, and as such, researchers should provide evidence regarding the nature and strength of the reliability and validity of any scale, test, assessment, or dependent variable used in a study—is the scale performing well in the sample being studied, do the scale's scores truly reflect the construct that researchers wish to measure? The second issue is the implications that scales' reliability and validity have for analysis and psychological implications. Among their effects, reliability affects one's statistical results, and validity affects one's ability to interpret results in terms of specific psychological phenomena.

Without proper understanding of the psychometric properties of the measures in a given study, researchers and readers cannot be sure that those measures were used and interpreted appropriately. Despite this importance, fundamental psychometric information is sometimes omitted from research reports. Unfortunately, we cannot assume confidently that the reliability of a scale's scores in one study or with one sample of participants generalizes to all studies or all samples. Thus, each time a scale is used, its scores should be evaluated in terms of psychometric quality. This volume and others (Nunnally & Bernstein, 1994; Furr & Bacharach, 2008) provide broad backgrounds for addressing psychometric quality.

Reliability can often be estimated quite easily for multi-item scales, and researchers usually assume that validity evidence generalizes across similar samples of participants. However, both of these practices are limited, as discussed later.

Dimensionality

A scale's dimensionality, or factor structure, reflects the number and nature of variables assessed by its items. Some questionnaires, tests, and inventories are unidimensional, with items cohering and reflecting a single psychological variable. Other questionnaires are multidimensional, with sets of items reflecting different psychological variables.

Usually based upon factor analysis, an accurate understanding of the number and nature of a scale's dimensionality directly affects its scoring, psychometric quality, and psychological meaning. Dimensionality dictates the number of meaningful scores that a scale produces for each participant. If a scale includes two independent dimensions, its items should be scored to reflect those dimensions. For example, the Positive Affect Negative Affect Schedule (PANAS; Watson et al., 1988) is a multidimensional questionnaire that produces one score for Positive Affect (PA) and another for Negative Affect (NA). Researchers typically do not combine items across the two dimensions, as it would produce scores reflecting no coherent psychological variable. By dictating the number of meaningful scores derived from a questionnaire, dimensionality also directs researchers' evaluations of reliability and validity. That is, researchers must understand the psychometric quality of *each* score obtained from a questionnaire. For example, the PANAS has been developed and used with psychometric attention to each of its two "subscales." Thus, researchers who develop and use psychological scales must understand the dimensionality of those scales. This is true even for short scales that might appear to reflect a single psychological variable. Inaccurate understanding of dimensionality can produce scores that are empirically and psychologically meaningless.

An important related point is that a scale's dimensionality is not clearly reflected by the familiar Cronbach's coefficient alpha. Based upon a scale's internal consistency, alpha is an estimate of a scale's reliability; however, it is not an index of unidimensionality. That is, a large alpha value cannot be interpreted as clear evidence of unidimensionality (see Chapter 4).

Finally, there are several recommendations that contradict many applications of factor analysis in evaluating the dimensionality of psychological scales. One is that the "eigenvalue greater than one" rule is a poor way to evaluate the number of dimensions underlying a scale's items; other procedures, such as scree plots, are preferable. A second recommendation is that oblique rotations are preferable to orthogonal rotations. These recommendations are detailed in Chapter 4.

Ad Hoc Scales

Occasionally, researchers create scales to measure specific constructs for a study. Of course, scale-development is important for psychological research, and there are good reasons to create new scales (e.g., one might wish to measure a construct for which a scale has not yet been developed). However, there are two caveats related to ad hoc scales.

The first caveat is that previously-validated scales are generally preferable to ad hoc scales. That is, when well-validated scales exist for a given construct, researchers should strongly consider using those scales rather than a new scale. For example, there are many well-validated self-esteem scales differing in length, psychological breadth, and dimensionality. With such diversity and known psychometric quality within easy reach, there seems little reason to assemble a new ad hoc self-esteem scale.

The second caveat is that, if ad hoc scales are created, they require psychometric evaluation, including validity evidence that goes beyond face validity. Ideally, scales that are intended to measure important psychological variables are developed through a rigorous process emphasizing psychometric quality. However, ad hoc scales sometimes seem to be applied without much evaluation, with researchers apparently relying upon on face validity and assuming that items obviously reflect the intended construct. Not only should researchers examine the dimensionality and reliability of ad hoc scales, but they should strive to obtain and report independent evidence of validity. For example, researchers might recruit independent raters (e.g., colleagues or students) to read the items along with items intended to reflect other variables, ask the raters to rate the clarity with which each item reflects each of several variables, and evaluate the degree to which each item was rated as clearly reflecting its intended variable. Such examinations produce validity-related evidence that goes beyond the researcher's opinions, and they might convince readers that a scale is sufficiently valid for narrowly-focussed application.

Modified Scales

In addition to creating ad hoc scales, researchers sometimes modify existing scales for new purposes. For example, researchers might shorten an existing scale or might revise a measure of one variable (e.g., health locus of control) to "fit" a different variable (e.g., financial locus of control). Again, there can be good reason for such modifications (e.g., existing scales are perceived as too lengthy, or there is no existing measure of the variable in question).

However, there are caveats that arise with modified scales, paralleling those associated with ad hoc scales and arising from the fact that modified scales might not have the psychometric properties or quality of an original scale. Indeed, the more substantially-modified a scale is, the less it can be assumed to have psychometric quality similar to the original. Thus, one caveat is that well-validated, original scales are preferable to modified scales. Because a modified scale's psychometric properties and quality might differ from those of the original scale, the modified scale is—to some degree—an ad hoc scale. As such, its psychometric properties and quality are unclear and suspect. Consequently, a second caveat is that modified scales require psychometric evaluation and interpretation. Because the psychometric properties of a modified scale likely differ from those of the original, researchers should carefully examine the scale's dimensionality, reliability, and validity.

Brief or Single-item Scales

An issue related to the creation or modification of scales is the use of brief scales—scales with very few items, perhaps only a single item. Indeed, brief scales are appealing, particularly when participants cannot be burdened with long scales.

Unfortunately, brief scales have important psychometric costs—their psychometric quality might be, likely *is*, poor or even unknown. As we shall see, traditional reliability theory suggests that reliability is relatively weak for brief scales, all else being equal. For example, recent research (van Dierendonck, 2005) compared three versions of a "Purpose in Life" scale—a 14-item version, a 9-item version, and a 3-item version. Results showed weaker reliability for shorter versions, with reliability estimates of $\alpha = .84$, $\alpha = .73$, and $\alpha = .17$ for the three versions, respectively. The particularly-poor reliability of the 3-item version suggests that "it is troublesome if the scales are to be used as variables in correlational analysis. Low reliability diminishes the chance of finding significant correlations" (van Dierendonck, 2005, p. 634). In fact, low reliability is problematic not only for typical "correlational analyses" but for *any* analysis of group differences or associations (see Chapter 4). A second difficulty particular to single-item scales is that they preclude the use of internal consistency methods for estimating reliability (e.g., coefficient alpha). Because internal consistency methods are easier than most other methods of estimating reliability, single-item scales are often used without attention to psychometric quality. This is a serious problem, preventing researchers, reviewers, editors, and readers from knowing the quality of a measurement that, being based upon single-item scale, is inherently suspect. Thus, researchers who use single-item scales might examine test–retest studies in order to estimate the reliability of the scales.

Importantly, brief or even single-item scales *can* have psychometric properties sufficient for researchers facing strict constraints in measurement strategies. For example, the Single-Item Self-Esteem Scale has good test–retest reliability estimates, and it has strong convergent validity correlations with the widely-used Rosenberg Self-Esteem Inventory (Robins et al., 2001). Similarly, the Ten-Item Personality Inventory has good test–retest estimates of reliability for each of its 2-item scales, which have strong convergent validity correlations with longer measures of their constructs (Gosling et al., 2003). The important point is that brief scales are appropriate and useful when their psychometric properties are adequate, as demonstrated by solid empirical estimates.

Scale Use Across Psychologically-differing Groups

Researchers often assume that psychometric properties generalize across samples of participants, but this assumption is not always valid. Indeed, a scale's psychometric properties might be importantly different in differing groups, and this might be particularly problematic for research in which scales are transported across cultural groups. Whether due to group differences in the interpretations of words, question/items, instructions, or the general meaning of a set of items, it is possible that "the items of the scale do not similarly represent the same latent construct … across groups" (Tucker et al., 2006, p. 343). In such situations, the scale's psychological meaning differs across groups and "the accuracy of interpretations about group differences on the latent construct is compromised" (ibid.).

Several considerations are important when a scale is used in groups that might differ psychologically from the group in which it was initially developed and validated. First, psychometric properties should be examined within each new group, and psychometric differences should be examined, understood, and potentially rectified before scores are used in those groups. If the new group might differ in the interpretation of a scale or in terms of the scale's link to the construct of interest, then researchers should explore this possibility. Results will either reveal that the scale is similarly meaningful in the new group, or they will reveal psychologically-interesting differences.

To establish the comparability of a scale across groups, researchers examine "test bias" (see Chapter 6), "measurement invariance," or differential item functioning (see Chapter 10). For example, Tucker et al. (2006) examined the Satisfaction With Life Scale (SWLS) in North Americans and Russians, finding that scores were not strongly comparable across groups. Such results suggest that comparison of groups' averages might produce misleading conclusions.

The second consideration is that careful translation does not guarantee psychometric stability across groups. Many researchers should be commended for careful attention in translating scales into a new language. Indeed, such attention is crucial for good cross-cultural work; however, it does not guarantee that the scale's psychometric properties or meaning are comparable. Again, the comparability of scale's properties, and ultimately of its psychological meaning, are revealed through psychometric analysis of responses to the scale.

Difference Scores

One important topic addressed in this volume is the use of difference scores as indicators of psychological phenomena. Difference scores—or "change scores" or "discrepancy scores"—are obtained by measuring two component variables and computing the difference between the two. For example, a participant's intergroup bias might be measured by having her rate the positivity of an ingroup and of an outgroup, and then calculating the difference between the two ratings. The difference might be interpreted as the degree to which she has a more favorable attitude toward the ingroup than toward the outgroup.

Difference scores are appealing, but their intuitive appeal masks complexities that have been debated for decades. Although much debate highlights the supposed unreliability of difference scores, there is also concern that difference scores can lack discriminant validity, in terms of simply reflecting one of their component variables. Both issues can compromise the psychological conclusions based upon difference scores.

This volume discusses these complexities, including psychometrically-based and statistically-based recommendations for handling them. First, and most generally, alternatives to difference scores should be considered seriously. That is, difficulties might be handled best by avoiding difference scores altogether, focussing instead on their component variables. Second, if difference scores are used, they should be used with attention to their components and to their psychometric quality. There seems to be a tendency to ignore the fact that difference scores are variables with psychometric properties that must be understood and considered when drawing psychological conclusions. Without such understanding and consideration, research based upon difference scores is ambiguous in terms of measurement quality, statistical validity, and psychological meaning.

Advanced Psychometric Perspectives

Advanced psychometric perspectives or tools such as Confirmatory Factor Analysis, Generalizability Theory, and Item Response Theory are increasingly accessible. As they become more well-known and well-integrated into user-friendly statistical software, they may become more important for scale development and evaluation.

Such perspectives offer important differences from and advantages over traditional psychometric theory, and they can be useful for understanding and evaluating the psychometric properties of psychological measures. Furthermore, producers and consumers of psychological research should be prepared to provide and/or interpret information obtained from these perspectives. Given the advantages of these perspectives, they may be the optimal choices for some—perhaps much—of the work in scale development and evaluation. This volume presents important principles of these perspectives, with examples that lay foundations for conducting and interpreting these important psychometric perspectives.

Steps in Scale Construction

Scale construction can be seen as a four-step process that is often iterative (Figure 2.1). Although each step is important, some are ignored in some scale construction procedures. Unfortunately, bypassing any of these steps might produce a scale with unknown psychometric quality and ambiguous meaning. High-quality research requires serious attention to scale construction and evaluation.

Step 1: Articulate the Construct and Context

The first, and perhaps most deceptively-simple, facet of scale construction is articulating the construct(s) to be measured. Whether the construct (one or more) is viewed as an attitude, a perception, an attribution, a trait, an emotional response, a behavioral response, a cognitive response, or a physiological response, or—more generally, a psychological response, tendency, or disposition of any kind—it must be carefully articulated and differentiated from similar constructs. Is more than one construct to be measured? What is the exact psychological definition of each construct? Is each construct narrow or broad? Does the construct have subcomponents or dimensions that should be differentiated and measured? What are the likely associations and differences between the intended construct and other relevant psychological constructs? Such questions guide subsequent steps in scale construction and evaluation, ultimately determining the scale's meaning and quality. For example, if an intended construct is not clearly differentiated from other constructs, then subsequent steps might produce a scale with poor validity and ambiguous meaning.

In addition, researchers creating a new scale must articulate the context in which it is likely to be used. The context includes at least two elements—the likely target population and the likely administration context. Obviously, the intended population will direct subsequent steps of item writing. For example, the response formats, items, or instructions for a scale intended to be used with adults would differ dramatically from those for one intended to be used with children. As discussed earlier, researchers cannot assume that a scale developed for and validated within one population is psychometrically comparable or similarly meaningful in different populations. Similarly, the likely administration context(s) must be considered carefully. For example, if the scale will be used primarily in research contexts that are time-sensitive, then subsequent steps will likely focus on brevity. Or, for example, if the scale will be administered via an online survey, then researchers should consider implementing online strategies in Step 3 of the construction process.[1]

Step 2: Choose Response Format and Assemble Initial Item Pool

In the second step of scale construction, researchers choose a response format and assemble an initial item pool. Guided by considerations from the first step, researchers write or seek out items that seem psychologically relevant to the intended construct. Of course, this depends on factors such as the number of constructs to be measured, the intended length of the scale, and the clarity of the construct's definition.

As discussed in Chapter 3, this step often includes iterative sub-steps in which items are discussed, considered in terms of conceptual relevance and linguistic clarity, and discarded or revised. In addition, this work may lead researchers to revisit the first step—potentially re-conceptualizing the focal construct(s). Indeed, a thoughtful item-writing process can reveal shortcomings in a scale's conceptual basis.

Step 3: Collect Data

After one or more constructs have been articulated, the likely assessment context has been determined, and items have been assembled, the items should be administered to respondents representing the likely target population, in a manner reflecting the likely administration context. This step has at least two purposes. First, it can reveal obvious problems through respondent feedback or observation. For example, respondents might require more time than initially supposed, or they might express confusion or frustration. Such issues might require revision of the scale. Second, this step produces data for the next step of scale construction— evaluation of the item pool's psychometric properties and quality.

Step 4: Psychometric Analysis

Scale construction requires attention to the psychometric properties of proposed items and of the proposed scale as a whole. By collecting data in a representative administration context and attending to dimensionality, reliability, and validity, researchers enhance the possibility that the scale will be useful and psychologically informative. Without such attention, even scales with the most straightforward appearance might be psychologically ambiguous or meaningless. Subsequent chapters articulate principles and processes important for psychometric evaluation.

The results of psychometric analyses determine subsequent phases of scale construction. If analyses reveal clear psychometric properties and strong psychometric quality, then researchers might confidently complete scale construction. However, psychometric analyses often reveal ways in which scales could be improved, leading researchers back to item (re)writing. In addition, psychometric analyses occasionally even lead researchers to re-conceptualize the nature of the construct(s) at the heart of the scale. Upon rewriting, the newly-revised scale should be evaluated in terms of its psychometric properties. This back-and-forth process of writing, analysis, and re-writing might require several iterations, but the result should be a scale with good psychometric quality and clear psychological meaning.

General Issue: Scale of Measurement

One general issue that sometimes escapes scrutiny is whether a scale produces scores at an interval level of measurement. At an interval level of measurement, the underlying psychological difference between scores is constant across the entire range of scores. Consider a hypothetical 1-item scale measuring homophobia: "I avoid homosexual people," with response options of *1 = Never, 2 = Rarely, 3 = Sometimes, 4 = Often, 5 = Always.* To interpret scores at an interval level of measurement, researchers must believe that the size of the psychological difference (in terms of underlying homophobic attitudes) between "Never" and "Rarely" avoiding homosexual people is identical to the size of the psychological difference between "Rarely" and "Sometimes" avoiding homosexual people. That is, the psychological difference between a score of 1 and a score of 2 is identical to the psychological difference between a score of 2 and a score of 3. There is serious debate about whether this is true for many psychological scales.

Level of measurement can have implications for the meaningfulness of specific forms of statistical analysis, though there is disagreement about this. Strictly speaking, a scale that is not at least at the interval level of measurement is difficult to interpret in terms of analyses based upon linear regression (as are ANOVA-based procedures). For example, an unstandardized regression slope reflects the difference in an outcome variable associated with a one-unit difference in a predictor variable. The psychological meaning of this is clear only when "a one-unit difference in a predictor variable" is consistent across levels of that variable. This is true for interval scales, but not for ordinal or nominal scales.

Regardless of ambiguities and disagreements, researchers generally treat Likert-type scales (such as the hypothetical homophobia scale) as an interval level of measurement. Particularly for aggregated scores obtained from multi-item scales, researchers assume that scores are "reasonably" interval-level. For very brief or single-item scales, this assumption is more tenuous. In such cases, researchers should either consider alternative analytic strategies or acknowledge the potential problem.

Summary

This chapter has reviewed principles and recommendation for scale construction, evaluation, and use, and has summarized the scale construction process. The remainder of this volume provides greater depth into the process, principles, and practices, hopefully enhancing motivation and ability to pursue effective measurement procedures.

Note

1   The possibility that online surveys differ meaningfully from traditional methods has received some empirical attention. For example, Gosling et al. (2004) found that web-based surveys produce results similar to those produced by traditional methods; however, they note that "this question has yet to be resolved conclusively" (p. 102).

3

Response Formats and Item Writing

Good research in social/personality psychology depends upon good measurement, which often depends upon careful and effective scale construction. This chapter focusses on the second step of the scale-construction process—choosing a response format and assembling items. Due to space limitations, it discusses key issues, but additional details are available in other excellent sources. Some sources provide general perspectives (e.g., John & Benet-Martinez, 2000; Wegener & Fabrigar, 2004; Dunn, 2009), with others focussing on specific domains (e.g., Jackson, 1971; Burisch, 1984; Fabrigar et al., 2006).

This chapter addresses scale construction in terms of scales common to lab-based research—multi-item questionnaires or inventories reflecting one or a few psychological variables. Such scales usually include either questions to be answered by respondents or statements to which respondents rate their level of agreement or endorsement, with items often framed in terms of agreement (e.g., with a statement of opinion or fact), frequency (e.g., of a behavior or event), quality (e.g., of an object), likelihood (e.g., of an event), truth (e.g., of an assertion), or importance (e.g., of a belief). To produce wide-ranging surveys for large-scale social or political research, such narrowly-targeted scales can be combined with other scales of varying content and format.

More specifically, this chapter focusses on scales with closed-ended items, which provide a limited number of response options. For example, true–false items, multiple-choice items, Likert-type items, and semantic differential items are all closed-ended items because respondents must choose from a set of pre-specified response options. Such items are common in psychological research, and they differ from open-ended items that place no or few constraints on responses (e.g., questions that elicit narrative responses). Other sources discuss considerations in designing open-ended items or wide-ranging social surveys (e.g., Chapter 6 in Dunn, 2009; Wegener & Fabrigar, 2004; Chapter 11 in Whitley, 2002; Visser et al., 2000).

Table 3.1   Considerations and recommendations in choosing a response format and assembling items

Considerations and recommendations
Response format
1   General type of format (e.g., likert, semantic-differential)
2   Number of options
3   Labels/anchors
4   Mid-points
5   "No opinion" and "Don't know"
6   Consistency across items
Item-writing
1   Relevant content
2   Number of items
3   Clear language (e.g., jargon, double-negatives, double-barreled)
4   Not leading or presumptive
5   Balanced scales—positively-keyed and negatively-keyed items

Response Formats

Roughly speaking, a scale's response format refers to the way in which items are presented and responses are obtained. As summarized in Table 3.1, there are several issues associated with response formats.

General type of format

As mentioned earlier, this discussion focuses on closed-ended scales. More specifically, it focusses on scales having graded response formats—scales generally described as Likert scales or semantic differential scales. These are probably the most common response formats in social/personality psychology.

For Likert-type scales, respondents read an item's text, which is usually a question or statement (e.g., "I like to go to parties"). They then choose one of the available response options (e.g., "Strongly Agree"). Usually, each available response option is associated with a specific quantitative value (e.g., 1 = Strongly Disagree; 5 = Strongly Agree), which are summed or averaged across all of a person's responses relevant to a given dimension.

In scales modeled on a semantic-differential format, each item includes paired adjectives representing the poles of a psychological dimension relevant to the construct of interest. For example, a measure of friendliness might include "cruel" and "kind," along with terms and/or values representing the breadth of the dimension (e.g., 1 = very cruel, 2 = somewhat cruel, 3 = equally cruel and kind, 4 = somewhat kind, 5 = very kind). Respondents consider the target of the assessment (e.g., themselves) and choose the appropriate term or value (note that, even if the options are not presented with numerical values, they are scored as having specific numerical values). Again, a participant's response values are aggregated across all adjective pairs relevant to a given dimension.

Number of response options

Researchers must consider the number of response options available to participants. A minimum of two is required (e.g., Agree/Disagree, True/False), but a larger number has benefits and costs. A potential benefit is that a relatively large number of options allows for finer gradations—potentially revealing subtler psychological differences among respondents than is possible with scales having few options. For example, a scale with response options that include "strongly agree," "moderately agree," and "slightly agree" (versus similar options of disagreement) allows participants to express *degrees* of agreement, whereas a dichotomous agree-versus-disagree scale does not. The potential cost of having many response options is potentially increased random error, as participants attempt to interpret overly-subtle gradations in the response format. In practice, researchers often use five or seven response options, balancing fine-gradation, subtlety, and psychometric quality.

Labels/anchors for response options

A third issue is the labeling of response options. Response options are often presented in terms of numerical values, and researchers must decide whether to supply verbal labels for some or all options. For example, researchers using a 7-point agreement format would, at minimum, label the endpoints (e.g., as strongly disagree and strongly agree). In addition, they might label one or more of the remaining points.

Research supports fully-labeled response options. That is, research reveals that labeling all response options produces better psychometric quality than does labeling only the endpoints, but there are limits to this benefit (Krosnick et al., 2005). For example, researchers will likely have difficulty providing clear, effective, widely-understood labels for a large number of response options. With a large number of response options, researchers might use terms like "somewhat agree," "mildly agree," "agree," and "strongly agree" to differentiate shades of agreement. However, such differentiation might not be clear to respondents, or might not be interpreted similarly by all respondents—one person's "somewhat agree" might be psychologically equivalent to another person's 'mild agreement.' Such ambiguity suggests that full-labeling of scales with more than six or seven response options might create more confusion than clarity.

Researchers labeling multiple response options should consider several straightforward yet practical issues. Labels should clearly differentiate the psychological meaning of the options. In addition, they should represent psychologically-equal differences among the response options, as much as possible (see

Chapter 2's comments regarding interval level of measurement). For example, the first three options might be labeled "Very Strongly Disagree = 1," "Strongly Disagree = 2," and "Mildly Disagree = 3." Unfortunately, the psychological difference between the first two options may be smaller than the psychological difference between the second and third options, and thus the labels should be revised. Finally, the labels should represent a broad range of the dimension being assessed. For example, response labels for an agreement scale should represent a broad range of "levels of agreement."

Mid-points

Following from the previous issues, the use of psychologically-neutral mid-points in a set of response options is a frequent consideration in scale construction. For example, an "agreement" scale might include an option reflecting a neutral, unde-cided, or non-committed level of agreement (versus disagreement). In terms of labels, mid-points are presented with terms such as "neutral" or "neither agree nor disagree." Alternatively, a scale might not include a neutral point, providing options referring only to various degrees of agreement or disagreement. A psycho-logical mid-point is often achieved through an odd-number of response options— e.g., a 5-point scale has a natural mid-point, whereas a 4-point scale does not.

There may be costs associated with psychological mid-points. Specifically, mid-points might be an "easy way out" for respondents who are unmotivated or unable to think carefully about the scale. Thus, mid-points might elicit less psychologically-informative or less accurate responses from some participants. Indeed, some researchers avoid mid-points, hoping to thereby "force respondents to go one way or the other"—for example, forcing participants to either agree or disagree with items.

However, the potential costs of mid-points are likely offset by important benefits, and—on balance—there is often good reason to use them. When participants do have genuinely-neutral responses to specific items, mid-points allow those responses, thereby enhancing the psychological accuracy of scale scores. Additionally and perhaps relatedly, some evidence suggests that the use of mid-points enhances scales' psychometric quality (O'Muircheartaigh et al., 2000). In this research, when mid-points were unavailable, people having truly-neutral psychological positions were forced to choose inaccurate options.

"No opinion" and "Don't know" response options

In some domains of psychology, researchers might wish to accommodate respondents who have no opinion regarding an item or who might not know their true psychological perspective regarding the item. Thus, researchers might con-sider "No opinion" or "Don't know" response options.

Some researchers might thus be tempted to label mid-point response options as "I don't know," to allow responses from people who might claim no knowledge or opinion regarding an item; however, this practice is inadvisable. For example, a person taking an attitude scale might have a carefully-considered opinion that is genuinely neutral, reflecting a thoughtful recognition of good and bad qualities of the attitudinal object. Such well-considered, genuinely neutral opinions are meaningfully different from a lack of opinion or a lack of knowledge, as would be reflected in a "No opinion" or "Don't know" response. Indeed, empirical analysis of mid-points and "Don't know" responses suggests that treating "Don't know" responses as a psychological mid-point compromises psychometric quality (O'Muircheartaigh et al., 2000). Thus, researchers should avoid treating a "No opinion" or "Don't know" response as being midway between two poles of the underlying psychological dimension.

More generally, a recent review of empirical work regarding "No opinion" and "Don't know" response options suggests that such options (even as separate from mid-points) are inadvisable (Krosnick et al., 2005). When they are available and respondents choose them, those choices seem to reflect issues other than genuine lack of knowledge or opinion. Rather, they reflect issues such as low motivation, genuine ambivalence about an object, or ambiguity in the question itself.

Considering these problems, the best solution is to create scales that have simplicity, clarity, and breadth of the underlying psychological dimension. For example, researchers might construct easily-read scales that minimize respondent fatigue, which might otherwise generate low motivation to respond thoughtfully. Similarly, they can write items that are as clear and simple as possible, reducing confusion or frustration. Finally, researchers should again make sure that response options reflect a broad range of the underlying dimension, potentially capturing nuanced perspectives of people with ambivalence toward the topic of the assessment.

Consistency across items

When constructing a psychological scale, researchers should consider at least two issues regarding the consistency of response options across items. First and perhaps most obviously, a scale's items should have equal numbers of response options. This is important because typical scoring procedures require researchers to sum or average across scale items, with all items equally weighted. Equal weighting is most likely to occur when items have equal numbers of response options. The second consideration is that the logical order of the response options should be consistent across items. For example, if one item's responses are ordered "Strongly Disagree," "Disagree," "Neutral," "Agree," and "Strongly Agree" (from left to right or from top to bottom), then all items' response options should be ordered similarly. If the order differs across items, then respondents might misread the scale and, consequently, provide inaccurate responses. Researchers rightly worry about respondents' motivation, attention, and ability to respond thoughtfully to item content, and the use of consistently-ordered response options eliminates one factor that might compromise these.

Assembling and Writing Items

Along with choosing a response format, researchers must assemble the scale's items—either by borrowing or modifying items from other scales or by writing new items. The current section presents suggestions for writing effective items (or for borrowing/modifying items).

Relevant content

Most fundamentally and obviously, items' content must reflect the intended psychological variable. This, of course, requires researchers to have a clear definition and understanding of the variable in question (Step 1 in the scale construction process) and to let this understanding guide item-writing. In addition, across all items, the breadth of the variable must be reflected in the scale's content. Many important psychological constructs are broad in scope, having several facets or modes of manifestation. For example, researchers intending to measure Extraversion might conceptualize it in terms of behavioral, cognitive, motivational, affective, and physiological components. If so, then their items should reflect all of these components. In contrast, the researchers might intend to measure only the behavioral component of Extraversion. Such a scale would not include item content reflecting the other components; however, it would be a measure of the behavioral component of Extraversion, not of Extraversion more broadly.

Number of items

A second important issue in assembling items is the number of items. Researchers must consider this issue for each construct to be measured by the scale, with each having its own set of items and receiving its own score. The optimal number of items depends upon several issues. First, traditional psychometric theory suggests that, all else being equal, longer scales have better reliability than shorter scales. Second, scales intended to reflect broadly-defined constructs may require more items than do scales reflecting narrowly-defined constructs. That is, to capture broad constructs such as Extraversion or Psychological Well-Being with good reliability and sufficient content-coverage, scales are likely to require a relatively large number of items. Although brief scales of some broad constructs have been developed, such scales are generally developed with rigorous attention to psychometric criteria, and they do not provide multidimensional information about the separate facets of the constructs. A third consideration in determining an optimal number of items is the likely context of administration (again, Step 1 of the scale construction process). As discussed earlier, a scale that is likely to be administered in time-sensitive contexts might need to be shorter than would otherwise be preferred.

Procedures presented later in this volume allow researchers to evaluate costs and benefits of different numbers of items, thereby enhancing scales' efficiency. For example, item-analysis, the Spearman–Brown prophecy formula, and Generalizability Theory allow researchers to identify good or bad items and to forecast the likely psychometric quality of scales of differing lengths. Such information, obtained in Step 4 of the scale construction process, is extremely useful when deciding whether to revise a scale and, if so, how to do so.

Clarity of language

To enhance the likelihood that participants will provide meaningful information, researchers should avoid things that reduce their motivation and ability to do so. Perhaps the most important such task is generating items that are easily-understood by potential respondents. Items and instructions that are relatively clear and simple are likely to be understood by respondents and to require little cognitive effort, enhancing respondents' ability and motivation to provide psychologically-meaningful responses.

There are several strategies for maintaining clear language in a scale's items. One fundamental recommendation is to avoid complex words (considering the likely target population), including psychological jargon. A second recommendation is to avoid double-negatives. For example, a Conscientiousness scale intended for students might include either of two items—"I never fail to do my homework" or "I always do my homework." Of course, most (hopefully all) students could understand the first item; however, doing so likely requires expending more cognitive effort than would be required by the second item. Consequently, the double-negative (i.e., "never" and "fail") of the first item might begin to diminish respondents' motivation and ability to complete the scale with care and accuracy, and several such items might cause problems for many respondents. Third, researchers should avoid double-barreled items—items reflecting two separable questions or statements. For example, another problematic potential Conscientiousness item might read, "I feel ashamed when I perform poorly on a test, therefore I avoid telling my parents about it." Specifically, what is the appropriate response from someone who feels ashamed about performing poorly, but who does tell his or her parents? Or what is the appropriate response from someone who avoids telling his or her parents about a poor performance, but who *does* so for reasons *other than* shame? The answers might be clear with some thought, but once again, such items place unnecessary cognitive demands on respondents. Thus, double-barreled items introduce confusion and, potentially, error into the scale.

Not leading or presumptive

The hypothetical Conscientiousness item "I feel ashamed when I perform poorly on a test, therefore I avoid telling my parents about it" reflects an additional subtle problem. Specifically, it presumes that a respondent performs poorly on tests, at least occasionally. That is, the item reads "… when I perform poorly on a test …," but some student respondents might not perform poorly on tests. What is the appropriate response from such students—disagreement with the statement, a neutral answer, a refusal to answer? Each of these responses creates ambiguity or missing data. For example, disagreements made by students who never perform poorly would be inseparable from: a) disagreements made by students who perform poorly but do not feel ashamed; or from b) disagreements made by students who perform poorly and who feel ashamed, but who do not avoid telling their parents.

Balanced scales

As a general rule, scales should be 'balanced' by including positively-keyed and negatively-keyed items. Positively-keyed items are those for which agreement or endorsement indicates a high level of the psychological variable being assessed. For example, the item "On the whole, I am satisfied with myself" is a positively-keyed item on the Rosenberg Self-esteem Scale—a genuine endorsement (i.e., a response of "Agree" or "Strongly Agree") reflects a high level of self-esteem, and rejection reflects lower self-esteem. In contrast, negatively-keyed items are those for which agreement or endorsement indicates a low level of the psychological variable. For example, the item "At times, I think I am no good at all" is a negatively-keyed item—genuine endorsement reflects a low level of self-esteem. Responses to negatively-keyed items must be reversed in the scoring process.

Balanced scales reduce the effects of acquiescence bias. As will be discussed (Chapter 6), acquiescence (or yea-saying) bias occurs when respondents agree to, or endorse items without regard for content, and nay-saying occurs when respondents disagree to, or refuse to endorse items without regard for content. Both biases can compromise the psychometric quality of scale scores, but balanced scales reduce the effects. Specifically, balanced scales reduce the possibility that relatively high (or low) scores will be obtained purely on the basis of acquiescence (or nay-saying). On balanced scales, participants responding purely with an acquiescent bias will obtain scores near the scale mid-point, which likely means that their scores will not create spuriously-large differences or positive (or negative) correlations. Without the use of balanced scales, researchers risk drawing inaccurate psychological conclusions from spuriously-large effects.

Summary

This chapter discussed two crucial facets of scale construction. When choosing response formats, researchers must consider issues such as the appropriate number of response options, the labeling of options, and the use of psychological mid-points. When writing items, they should consider issues such as the clarity of language, relevant content, and the use of balanced scales. Well-considered scale construction can increase the chance that respondents will complete the scale with proper motivation, good attention, and sufficient ability.

4

Evaluating Psychometric Properties: Dimensionality and Reliability

The fourth step of scale construction is examination of psychometric properties and quality. This step, though sometimes bypassed when creating ad hoc scales, is crucial. With a solid understanding of a scale's dimensionality, reliability, and validity, researchers can conduct research that provides clear information. Without such understanding, the meaning and quality of one's research is suspect.

This chapter and the next survey fundamental issues in evaluating scales' psychometric properties and quality. This chapter focusses on the interrelated issues of dimensionality and reliability of responses to a scale, and the next focusses on the validity with which a scale's scores are interpreted. Each provides a conceptual introduction to the topics, articulates their importance for psychological research, and provides practical guidance for conducting relevant psychometric evaluation.

Dimensionality

The meaning of dimensionality

As described earlier, a scale's dimensionality, or factor structure, refers to the number and nature of the variables reflected in its items. Researchers must consider several issues regarding a scale's dimensionality (see Figure 4.1). First, they must understand the number of psychological variables, or dimensions, reflected in its items. A scale's items might be unidimensional, all reflecting a single common psychological variable, or they might be multidimensional, reflecting two or more psychological variables. The second core dimensionality issue is, if a scale is multidimensional, whether the dimensions are correlated with each other. A robust correlation between dimensions suggests that the dimensions, though separable, share a deeper common psychological variable. The third dimensionality issue is, again if a scale is multidimensional, the psychological meaning of the dimensions. Researchers must identify the nature of the psychological variables reflected by the dimensions.

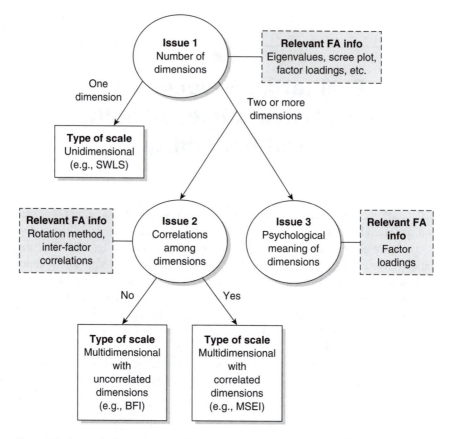

Figure 4.1   Issues in dimensionality, relevant elements of Exploratory Factor Analysis and types of scales

Importance of dimensionality

These issues reflect the nature of the scale (see Figure 4.1), which in turn determines its appropriate scoring, evaluation, and interpretation. The number of dimensions is important because each dimension should be scored separately, with each requiring psychometric evaluation. That is, each score obtained from a scale should reflect a single coherent psychological variable. If a score reflects a blend of non-correlated dimensions, then its psychological meaning is highly ambiguous. Thus, a unidimensional scale produces a single score representing the lone dimension reflected in its items; however, a multidimensional scale produces multiple scores—one for each dimension reflected in its items. The correlational pattern among the dimensions of a multidimensional scale is important in part because it has implications for the meaningfulness of combined scores or "total scores" for a multidimensional scale. Specifically, if dimensions are correlated robustly (reflecting some shared deeper psychological variable), then scores from those dimensions might be combined to form a score reflecting their shared psychological variable. For example, the Multidimensional Self-esteem Inventory (MSEI; O'Brien & Epstein, 1988) assesses several correlated dimensions of self-esteem, and the fact that the "Likability" and "Lovability" dimensions are correlated suggests that they share some common psychological meaning in terms of social self-esteem. Thus, those dimensions might be scored separately *and* combined to form a "Social Self-esteem" score. In contrast, if dimensions are uncorrelated, then their scores should not be combined. The third dimensionality issue—the psychological meaning of the dimensions—is important because a clear understanding of the scores' psychological meaning is necessary for the proper interpretation of scale scores and ultimately for the psychological implications of research based upon those scores.

Evaluating dimensionality

Exploratory Factor Analysis (EFA) is the most common method of evaluating the dimensionality of psychological scales, and this section summarizes EFA's logic, procedures, and interpretation. Several useful and accessible sources provide additional detail regarding factor analysis in general or in terms of scale construction (e.g., Floyd & Widaman, 1995; Thompson, 2004).

Conceptual overview   A scale's dimensionality is reflected in the correlations among its items, and EFA operates on those correlations to address the three key dimensionality issues. Conceptually, EFA scans the inter-item correlations, seeking sets of items—that is, it seeks groups of items that are relatively strongly correlated with each other but weakly correlated with other items. Each set of relatively highly-correlated items represents a psychological dimension or "factor." If all scale items are well-correlated with each other at approximately equal levels, then there is only a single set, and the scale is unidimensional. If, however, there are two or more sets, then the scale is multidimensional.

The potential correlations among dimensions arise from correlations between items in different sets. If items from one set are somewhat correlated with items from another set, then the factors represented by those sets are correlated with each other. If, however, items from one set are weakly-correlated or un-correlated with items from another, then the factors represented by those sets are uncorrelated with each other.

Finally, the content of the items comprising a set reflects the potential psychological meaning of the factor represented by that set. That is, the potential meaning of a factor arises from whatever its items appear to have in common. This is, of course, a matter of interpretation and judgment—one researcher's interpretation of the psychological essence of several items might differ from another's. EFA cannot decide this issue, but it distills information in a way that informs researchers' understanding and enhances their ability to make empirically-based judgments. In practice, the EFA process (see Figure 4.2) is iterative, as results of one step often lead researchers to re-evaluate previous steps.

Choosing an extraction method   The first step of EFA is choosing an extraction method, which refers to the statistical procedures to be used—e.g., Principal Axis Factoring (PAF), Maximum Likelihood Factor Analysis, Principal Components Analysis (PCA). The most popular choices are PAF and PCA. Technically, PCA is not "factor" analysis, though it is often described as such and is the default method for several popular statistical software packages' factor analysis procedure.

Indeed, PAF and PCA are based upon different statistical models. In PAF, responses to a scale's items are seen as arising from underlying psychological (latent) variables—for example, a person endorses a "talkativeness" item because he or she has a relatively high level of extraversion (or whatever the relevant underlying trait or state may be). In PCA however, the composites are seen as being weighted combinations of the items, and the goal is simply to account efficiently for variance in the items.

Although there is often little practical difference between PAF and PCA, many experts suggest that PAF (or another form of factor analysis) is usually the better option. For example, Fabrigar et al. (1999, p. 276) conclude that PCA is not recommended "[w]hen the goal of the analysis is to identify latent constructs underlying measured variables," as is the goal in scale construction. If PCA is conducted, then it should be described as "components analysis" rather than factor analysis, and results should be described in terms of components, not factors. For some statistical software, the choice of extraction method is the only decision required before proceeding to the next step.

Identifying the number of factors   The second step of EFA is identifying the number of factors underlying a set of items. There is no single, clear-cut criterion to inform this identification; rather, there are guidelines that can be used. Perhaps the most familiar are the "eigenvalue greater than one" rule and the scree test. Other guidelines (e.g., parallel analysis) are not currently integrated into popular statistical software.

Researchers should generally avoid using the "eigenvalue greater than one" guideline, because it "is *among the least accurate methods* for selecting the number of factors to retain" (Costello & Osborne, 2005, p. 2; italics in original). Unfortunately, this guideline is the default for some popular statistical packages. Researchers should override this default.

Thus, the scree plot is the best widely-available option for evaluating the number of factors underlying a set of items. A scree plot graphically presents the eigenvalues

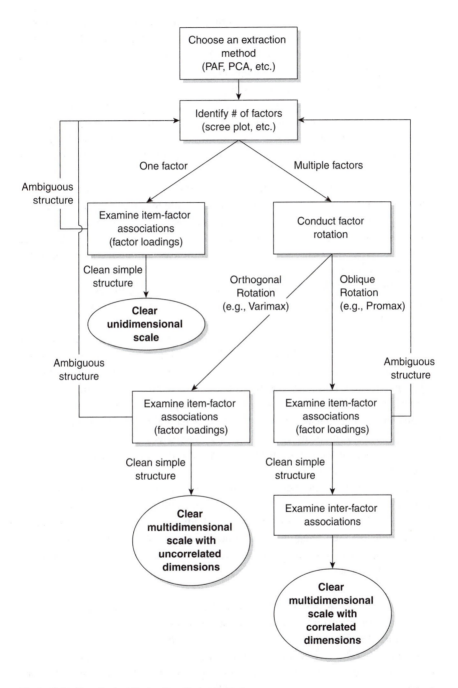

Figure 4.2   Flowchart of Exploratory Factor Analysis

associated with a factor analysis, highlighting their descending magnitudes. When interpreting a scree plot, researchers hope to find a clear "leveling-off point." For example, Figure 4.3a is a scree plot from a factor analysis of a hypothetical 7-item "Scale E," and it shows a clear flattening beginning at "factor 3." An obvious flattening point leads researchers to conclude that there are one less than the factor number of the flattened point. For Figure 4.3a, the flattening point is at factor 3, so the researcher would conclude that there are two factors. If there is a large drop from the first eigenvalue to the second, followed by a leveled-off line beginning at the second, then the research would likely conclude that the scale includes a single factor.

Unfortunately, scree plots are not always clear. If a scale's dimensionality is unclear or complex (e.g., in terms of correlated dimensions), then its scree plot might look more like Figure 4.3b (for a hypothetical "Scale N"). In this figure, the plot slopes downward without a clear leveling-off, providing little guidance. In such cases, researchers use additional information in order to understand the number of dimensions underlying the scale's items.

Thus, to some degree, decisions regarding the number of factors are often informed by the clarity of the item-factor associations. For example, on the basis of Figure 4.3b, researchers might (somewhat arbitrarily) decide to extract two factors and proceed to the next step of the analysis. As will be discussed, findings at subsequent steps might lead the researchers to return to this step, extract a different number of factors and proceed again to the next steps. They might continue to this second step, hoping to identify a number of factors that produce relatively clear results in terms of the item-factor associations. Occasionally, clarity never appears, indicating that there is no clear dimensionality for the scale. In such cases, researchers might need to revisit the first steps of the scale construction process—clarifying the nature of the constructs to be assessed and writing items that clearly reflect each construct.

If things go well, researchers reach an initial decision regarding the number of factors underlying a scale's items, and they proceed to one of two subsequent steps. If the scree plot (or another good guideline) indicates that items reflect a single dimension, then researchers examine the item-factor associations. However, if evidence indicates multiple dimensions, then researchers must make decisions regarding factor rotation.

Choosing how to rotate factors When working with items that appear multidimensional, researchers usually "rotate" factors. Rotation is intended to clarify the nature of the factors (which will be discussed shortly).

There are two basic kinds of rotation, with implications for potential associations among factors. Orthogonal rotations (e.g., Varimax) produce factors that are uncorrelated with each other, whereas oblique rotations (e.g., Promax) produce factors that might be correlated with each other (though not guaranteeing so). To

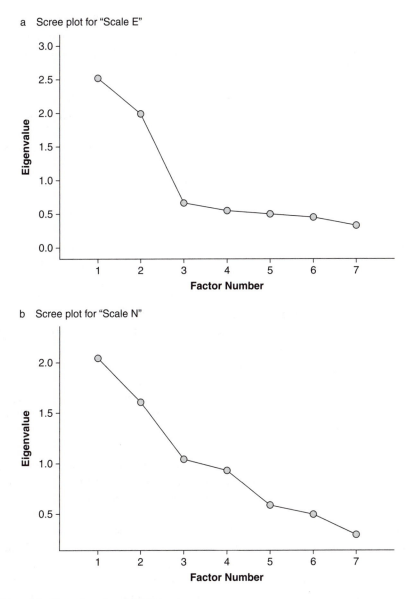

Figure 4.3   Examples of scree plots

anthropomorphize, if factors "want to be" correlated with each other, then oblique rotations allow them to be.

Many experts recommend oblique rotations over orthogonal. Indeed, there seems to be little conceptual or psychometric reason to impose orthogonality upon a scale's dimensions, and doing so can produce less clarity than would oblique rotations. Simply put, oblique rotations allow researchers to understand their scales most clearly. After rotating factors from an apparently-multidimensional scale, researchers attempt to identify the items linked to each factor.

Examining item-factor associations   A complete understanding of the psychological meaning of a scale's dimensions requires many kinds of information, and the links between items and factors are potentially important pieces of information. These links are reflected in values called factor loadings, with a separate loading reflecting the association between each item and each factor. By identifying the items most strongly linked to each factor, researchers begin to understand the nature of those factors.

Factor loadings generally range between -1 and $+1$ and are interpreted as correlations or standardized regression weights. Orthogonal rotations (and examinations of a single factor) produce loadings that can be seen as correlations between each item and each factor. Oblique rotations produce several kinds of factor loadings. For example, oblique rotations via SPSS produce "pattern coefficients" and "structure coefficients." Pattern coefficients are the standardized regression weights obtained from a regression equation in which respondents' item responses are predicted from their levels of the underlying factors. In contrast, structure coefficients are simply correlations between respondents' item responses and their levels of the underlying factors. Because they account for potential overlap/correlation between factors (in oblique rotations), pattern coefficients often provide sharper clarity about the unique associations between items and factors. When interpreting the magnitudes of factor loadings, many researchers consider loadings above .30 or .40 as reasonably strong, with loadings of .70 or .80 being very strong.

For example, Scale E's scree plot in Figure 4.3a strongly suggested a two-factor dimensionality; therefore, I extracted two factors, used an oblique rotation (i.e., "Promax"), and obtained the loadings in Figure 4.4a. This factor pattern matrix reveals that the first four items of this scale loaded strongly on Factor 1, with loadings >.70. Similarly, items 5, 6, and 7 loaded strongly on factor 2.

Generally, researchers sum or average a participant's responses to the items that load together on a factor. If an item does not load on a factor, then it should not be included in the scoring of the dimension reflected by that factor. For example, considering the clear two-dimensional results in Figures 4.3a and 4.4a, researchers would likely average (or sum) a participant's responses to the first four items of "Scale E" to create one score and they would average responses to the last three items to create another score.

With this goal in mind, researchers hope that factor loadings have a "simple structure" in which each item is strongly linked to one and only one factor. For example, the pattern matrix in Figure 4.4a has very clear, simple structure – each item loads strongly on one factor and very weakly on the other. In scale construction, simple structure clearly reveals which items should be aggregated together

4.4a

Pattern Matrix

	Factor	
	1	2
Eitem2	.713	−.085
Eitem4	.708	.023
Eitem1	.705	.055
Eitem3	.705	.007
Eitem5	.008	.726
Eitem7	.013	.707
Eitem6	−.021	.689

4.4b

Pattern Matrix

	Factor	
	1	2
Nitem2	.771	−.237
Nitem1	.725	.253
Nitem3	.670	−.024
Nitem6	.053	−.014
Nitem7	−.008	.971
Nitem5	−.051	.520
Nitem4	−.017	.107

4.4c

Factor Matrix

	Factor
	1
Nitem1	.844
Nitem3	.655
Nitem2	.600
Nitem7	.195
Nitem5	.100
Nitem6	.048
Nitem4	.016

4.4d

Pattern Matrix

	Factor		
	1	2	3
Nitem2	.798	−.217	.071
Nitem1	.702	.247	−.110
Nitern3	.670	−.007	.031
Nitem7	−.032	.937	−.030
Nitem5	−.025	.577	.154
Nitem4	.070	.196	.348
Nitem6	.019	−.044	−.133

4.4e

Pattern Matrix

	Factor	
	1	2
Nitem2	.768	−.234
Nitem1	.727	.257
Nitem3	.670	−.021
Nitem7	−.001	.985
Nitem5	−.044	.507

Figure 4.4   Examples of factor loading matrices

in order to form scores. Rotation enhances the chance that simple structure will emerge; therefore, rotation is a key part of most factor analyses.

There are two ways in which factor loadings can violate simple structure. First, an item might have weak loadings on all factors, and, second, an item might have strong loadings on multiple factors. For example, Figure 4.4b is a pattern matrix obtained from "Scale N" that produced the highly-ambiguous scree plot in Figure 4.3b. Because the scree plot was unclear, I arbitrarily began with a two-factor extraction and oblique rotation. As implied by the ambiguous scree plot, the resulting factor loadings do not reveal simple structure. Specifically, neither item 4 nor item 6 load on either factor. Thus, these items do not fit with the rest of the items. Moreover, items 2 and 3 load primarily on factor 1, but also have somewhat elevated loadings on factor 2. Although these secondary loadings (or "off-factor" loadings) are not strong, they begin to disrupt the clarity of the factor structure.

Researchers might opt to eliminate items with poor structure. A lack of association with all factors suggests that the item is not coherently related to the other items on the scale, suggesting that it represents a different psychological variable than do the other items (or that it is highly affected by random error). In such cases, the item does not belong on the scale (see also the discussion of internal consistency, below). In contrast, the existence of multiple robust factor loadings suggests that an item reflects more than one psychological variable—that responses to the item are driven by more than one psychological variable. In such cases, the item does not uniquely reflect either variable, and thus might need to be dropped or revised to reflect only one variable. Another option, aside from eliminating potentially-problematic items, is for researchers to re-visit their initial decision about the number of factors underlying the items.

Indeed, as mentioned earlier (see Figure 4.1), factor loadings can clarify the psychological meaning of a scale's dimensions, but they can also address the first dimensionality issue—the number of dimensions reflected in a scale's items. As noted earlier, scree plots do not always provide clear insight into this issue, but the clarity of the factor loadings provides additional guidance. For example, the scree plot in Figure 4.3b does not suggest a particular structure. In such cases, researchers might examine factor loadings based on several factor structures, examining the clarity and meaningfulness of each. If one set of results is clearer and more meaningful, then researchers might conclude that the "correct" number of factors is the one producing the clearest and most meaningful pattern of factor loadings. For example, Figures 4.4c and 4.4d reflect 1-factor and 3-factor matrices for "Scale N," which produced the unclear scree plot in 4.3b and the ambiguous 2-factor matrix in Figure 4.4b. Unfortunately neither of these is clearer. Thus, as a researcher, I would likely conclude that the items have a 2-factor structure that needs work—perhaps dropping items 4 and 6. In even further analyses, I might omit these items from the factor analysis and rerun everything. Doing this, I obtain a much clearer scree plot (not presented) and a two-factor pattern matrix with clearer simple structure (Figure 4.4e).

Examining associations among factors   Finally, researchers using oblique rotations must examine correlations among the factors. Oblique rotations produce a correlation for each pair of factors, revealing the "higher-order" structure of associations among factors. Such information is crucial to understanding the nature of the factors and to scoring the scale. As mentioned earlier, aggregation of multiple scale scores into a total score is reasonable only for scores representing robustly-correlated dimensions.

Reliability

The remainder of this chapter addresses the definition, importance, and estimation of reliability. It presents Classical Test Theory (CTT), which is the traditional basis of reliability in psychology and which provides a foundation for effective scale construction, measurement, and psychometric evaluation. The second half of this volume introduces new psychometric perspectives with potential advantages over CTT. This chapter focusses on issues most relevant for social/personality scales, with additional breadth and depth available elsewhere (e.g., Feldt & Brennan, 1989; Furr & Bacharach, 2008).

Meaning of reliability

Earlier, reliability was defined (roughly) as the precision of scale scores, but a better definition arises from several core concepts and from the notion that most psychological measurement is an attempt to capture psychological variability. Conceptually, reliability begins with assumptions about the components underlying scale scores.

Observed scores, true scores, and error   CTT rests on assumptions about the nature of scores obtained when people respond to a scale, test, or measure of any kind (i.e., the nature of "observed scores"). One assumption is that observed scores are additively determined by true score and measurement error:

$$O_X = T_X + E_X \qquad \text{(Equation 4.1)}$$

where O_X is a participant's observed score on a scale measuring variable X, T_X is the participant's true score, and E_X is the measurement error affecting his or her observed score.

True scores are the signal a researcher wishes to detect. A participant's true score is the score that he or she would obtain if the scale was perfectly precise— that is, if it was unaffected by measurement error. More technically, a true score is the average score that a participant would obtain if he or she completed the scale an infinite number of times. Some researchers equate (conceptually) a participant's

Table 4.1   Hypothetical data illustrating CTT

Participant	Observed Score (O_x)		True Score (T_x)		Measured Error (E_x)
Group 1					
1	33	=	36	+	−3
2	39	=	34	+	5
3	30	=	32	+	−2
4	28	=	30	+	−2
5	33	=	28	+	5
6	23	=	26	+	−3
Group 2					
7	28	=	31	+	−3
8	34	=	29	+	5
9	25	=	27	+	−2
10	23	=	25	+	−2
11	28	=	23	+	5
12	18	=	21	+	−3
Means (Var)					
Group 1	31(24.33)		31(11.67)		0(12.67)
Group 2	26(24.33)		26(11.67)		0(12.67)
Cohen's d	1.01		1.46		
t value	1.60		2.31		
p value	.14		.04		

true score with the participant's actual standing on the construct assessed by the scale, though this has been criticized.

If one views true scores as the signal to be detected, then measurement error is noise obscuring that signal. Measurement error inhibits researchers' ability to obtain accurate measurement of participants' true scores. A second key assumption of CTT is that measurement error is random, artificially inflating or deflating observed scores in a way that is unrelated to true scores or any other quality of the participants. That is, respondents with high true scores are no more (or less) likely to have their observed scores inflated or deflated by measurement error (e.g., being in an unusually good mood, or mistakenly marking "strongly agree" instead of "agree") than are respondents with lower true scores. Similarly, the factors that make a respondent's observed score higher than it should be during one assessment occasion might not affect his or her observed scores obtained during another assessment occasion. In sum, CTT conceptualizes "noise" in terms of unsystematic or random measurement error.

Consider the hypothetical "Group 1" data in Table 4.1—a conceptual example requiring us to assume temporary omniscience (i.e., we could not truly know all elements of this table). In these data, each observed score reflects true score plus error. Similarly, error scores reflect the "random" assumption—they are uncorrelated with true scores and they sum to zero. We will revisit these values to illustrate principles of CTT.

Detecting psychological variability Most psychological measurement is intended to reflect differences in a psychological attribute or action; that is, psychological measurement is typically intended to capture psychological variability. When researchers use the Rosenberg self-esteem scale, they typically are attempting to capture differences among participants' levels of self-esteem. That is, they wish to identify the participants who have relatively high self-esteem and those who have relatively low self-esteem, and they wish to quantify the degree of differences between participants' levels of self-esteem. Even in single-subject or repeated-measures research, psychological measurement hinges on the ability to detect psychological variability—specifically, variability within each participant as he, she, or it experiences psychological change across time, situations, or conditions. Finally, applied psychological measurement hinges on variability—whether attempting to identify the most capable, motivated, or qualified applicants or attempting to detect whether a patient exhibits psychological change, measurement is linked to psychological variability.

Given the importance of psychological variability, reliability hinges on variability in the context of observed scores, true scores, and error. Based upon Equation 4.1 and upon the assumption that error is random, variability in observed scores reflects variability in true scores and in error scores:

$$s^2_{O_X} = s^2_{T_X} + s^2_{E_X}$$ (Equation 4.2)

In this equation, $s^2_{O_X}$ is the variance of observed scores, $s^2_{T_X}$ is the variance of true scores, and $s^2_{E_X}$ is the variance of error scores. Typically, these values are conceptualized as between-person variances (e.g., the degree to which people have observed scores that differ from each other, the degree to which the individuals' true scores differ). Again, the hypothetical "Group 1" data in Table 4.1 illustrate these relationships: $24.33 = 11.67 + 12.67$, within rounding.

Defining reliability Just as psychological attributes such as self-esteem are unobserved properties of people, reliability is an unobserved property of scale scores. It is a theoretical quality, defined through theoretical terms such as true scores and measurement error.

Perhaps most commonly, reliability is defined as the degree to which observed score variance reflects true score variance, reflecting a ratio of signal and noise:

$$\text{Reliability} = \frac{\text{Signal}}{\text{Signal} + \text{Noise}}$$

In terms of true variance and error variance,

$$r_{XX} = \frac{s^2_{T_X}}{s^2_{T_X} + s^2_{E_X}} \text{ or } r_{XX} = \frac{s^2_{T_X}}{s^2_{O_X}}$$

Thus, reliability (r_{XX}) is the degree to which observed scores reflect mostly psychological signal (in terms of whatever variable is assessed by the scale), rather than noise. More technically, it is the proportion of variance in observed scores that is attributable to variance in true scores. As applied to the "Group 1" hypothetical data in Table 4.1, the reliability is .48:

$$r_{XX} = \frac{12.67}{24.33}$$

$$r_{XX} = .48$$

Thus, only 48 percent of the variability in observed scale scores is attributable to true score variability.

In fact, there are several ways of defining reliability. Although they reflect different perspectives on the same concept, they are statistically equivalent. For example, reliability can be seen as the degree to which differences in participants' observed scores are consistent with differences in their true scores:

$$r_{XX} = r^2_{O_X T_X}$$

where $r^2_{O_X T_X}$ is the squared correlation between participants' observed scale scores and their true scores. For the "Group 1" data in Table 4.1,

$$r_{XX} = r^2_{O_X T_X} = .69^2 = .48$$

In addition, reliability can be seen as the degree to which observed score variance is unaffected by error variance, and as the degree to which observed scores are uncorrelated with error scores.

Reliability ranges between 0 and 1, with larger values indicating greater psychometric quality. There is no clear cut-off separating good and poor reliability, but values of .70 or .80 are generally viewed as sufficient for research. As a producer and consumer of research, I worry when reliability falls below .70 or .60. Reliabilities below these values suggest significant psychometric problems, with important implications for statistical analyses and psychological conclusions.

Importance of reliability

Reliability is a crucial issue in scale construction and use. For applied psychology, it affects the accuracy with which an individual's observed scale score approximates his or her true score. Good reliability means that a person's scale score is a good estimate of his or her true score, and poor reliability means that a person's scale score might be dramatically discrepant from his or her true score. If scales or tests are used to inform decisions about an individual (e.g., college admission, class placement),

Table 4.2   The effect of reliability on effect sizes and inferential statistics in three common analytic contexts

Analytic context	Effect size	Inferential statistic
Association between variables	Correlation $r_{O_X O_Y} = r_{T_X T_Y} \sqrt{r_{XX} r_{YY}}$	t-test of correlation $t = \dfrac{r_{T_X T_Y} \sqrt{r_{XX} r_{YY}}}{\sqrt{1 - r_{T_X T_Y}^2 r_{XX} r_{YY}}} \sqrt{N-2}$
Group differences[a] (two groups)	Cohen's d $d_{O_X} = d_{T_X} \sqrt{r_{XX}}$	Independent groups t-test $t = d_{T_X} \sqrt{r_{XX}} \left(\dfrac{\sqrt{N-2}}{2} \right)$
Group differences (two or more groups)	Eta Squared $\eta_{O_X}^2 = \eta_{T_X}^2 r_{XX}$	F-test (e.g., ANOVA) $F = \dfrac{\eta_{T_X}^2 r_{XX}}{1 - \eta_{T_X}^2 r_{XX}} \left(\dfrac{df_{Error}}{df_{Effect}} \right)$

Note: [a]The reliability values in these equations refer to reliability within each group, assuming that the groups have equal reliability. This equation for an independent groups t-test is based on equal sample sizes.

then those scales or tests must have very strong reliability. For research (the context of interest for most readers of this volume), reliability is important because it affects the effect sizes—and consequently the statistical significance—of one's analyses.

Reliability and effect sizes   According to CTT, an observed effect size is determined by two factors: a) the true effect size, in terms of the effect that would be observed with perfect measurement of participants in the sample; and b) the reliability of the measure(s) completed by participants. In essence, the true effect size is what researchers wish to understand—what is the psychological effect or difference? Researchers analyze observed scale scores (and any other measured variables), using observed effect sizes as estimates of true effect sizes.

Table 4.2 summarizes reliability's influence on effect sizes for three types of research questions. Perhaps most familiar is its effect on associations between two measures (e.g., measures of variables X and Y). As shown in Table 4.2, the correlation between observed scores for two scales $\left(r_{O_X O_Y} \right)$ is determined by the true correlation (i.e., the correlation between true scores for the two scales, $r_{T_X T_Y}$) and the reliabilities of both scales (r_{XX}, r_{YY}).

Less familiar (but no less important) is reliability's effect on apparent differences between groups—a common research question among many psychologists. Table 4.2 shows these effects for a two-group context and for a two-or-more-group context.

In a two-group context, Cohen's d is often the effect size of interest, reflecting the standardized difference between group means. The "observed" effect size (d_{O_X}) is computed for two groups compared on observed scores for scale X, and it is determined by the true effect size (i.e., the d value for true scores, d_{T_x}) and the reliability of scale X (r_{xx}). To illustrate this concretely, Table 4.1 presents hypothetical two-group data reflecting the assumptions of CTT within each group and across groups. Although researchers do not know true scores (recall that these values are based upon temporary omniscience), this example reveals "true" group means of 31 and 26 and "true" within-group variances of 11.67. These values produce a large "true" d = 1.46, indicating that the "true" means are 1.46 standard deviations apart.[1] This is the effect size that researchers wish to detect. Now, note the means, variabilities, and effect size for the observed scores—values that researchers would actually obtain and use to inform their conclusions. The observed means are identical to the true means (due to the assumption that error is random, thus sums to zero across respondents), but observed score variances are considerably larger than true score variances (because observed score variances are inflated by error variance). Given the inflated within-group variabilities, the observed values produce a smaller d=1.01, indicating that the observed means are "only" 1 standard deviation apart. These values are consistent with the equation presented in Table 4.2:

$$d_{O_x} = 1.46\sqrt{.48}$$

$$d_{O_x} = 1.01$$

Thus, the observed effect is noticeably smaller than the true effect, and thus it is a poor estimate of the true effect. The difference between the true effect and the observed effect is due to measurement error (i.e., imperfect reliability).

In a two-or-more group context, the same principles apply. The eta-squared value observed for multiple groups measured on scale X ($\eta_{O_x}^2$) is determined by the true eta-squared value (i.e. the eta-squared value for the group means of the true scores, $\eta_{T_x}^2$) and the reliability of the scale (r_{XX}).

The example in Table 4.1 reveals that imperfect reliability attenuates observed effect sizes. That is, when examining scales that have imperfect reliability (as all measures do), the effects obtained by researchers underestimate the true effects. The degree of attenuation is determined by reliability—poorer reliability produces greater attenuation.

The attenuating effect of imperfect reliability is crucially important for at least two reasons. First, effect sizes are fundamental statistical information, providing important insight into the nature of those effects. Indeed, Cohen asserts that "the primary product of a research inquiry is one or more measures of effect size, not p values" (1990, p. 1310), and an increasing number of journals now require or encourage effect sizes. Researchers ignoring reliability risk misunderstanding the actual psychological effects in their research.

Although rarely done, researchers can use a "correction for attenuation" to estimate true effects. That is, if researchers have information about the reliability of their measures, then they can use their observed effects and rearrange the equations in Table 4.2 to estimate the true effects. For example, the correlational correction for attenuation is:

$$r_{T_X T_Y} = \frac{r_{O_X O_Y}}{\sqrt{r_{XX} r_{YY}}} \qquad \text{(Equation 4.3)}$$

Although researchers seem hesitant to use it, this correction makes psychometric sense according to CTT and can provide useful information. We will return to this in Chapter 6.

Reliability and statistical significance   The attenuating effect of imperfect reliability is also important because it affects statistical significance. Larger effect sizes produce a greater likelihood of obtaining "significant" results, while smaller effect sizes reduce this likelihood. Thus, through its influence on effect sizes, reliability affects the likelihood of obtaining significant results – good reliability enhances the likelihood and poor reliability reduces it.

Table 4.2 presents equations for three common inferential statistics, showing the influence of reliability and effect sizes. For each statistic—a t-test for a correlation, an independent groups t-test of two means, and an F-test of two or more group means—the "observed" inferential statistic is determined by the true effect size, the reliability of the scale scores (or tests, or any other measured variable), and the size of the study.

The hypothetical data in Table 4.1 illustrate these effects. Again, the true-score effect size of the group difference is 1.46, but the observed effect size is only 1.01. Given this true-score effect size and the sample size, the true-score group difference is statistically significant (because the equation below is based upon the true-scores, the reliability term is omitted):

$$t = 1.46 \left(\frac{\sqrt{12 - 2}}{2} \right)$$

$$t = 1.46(1.58)$$

$$t = 2.31, df = 10, p = .04$$

Thus, the "true story" is that the groups have significantly different means on variable X. However, based on the reliability $r_{XX} = .48$, the observed group difference is non-significant:

$$t = 1.46\sqrt{.48}\left(\frac{\sqrt{12}-2}{2}\right)$$

$$t = 1.01(1.58)$$

$$t = 1.60, \, df = 10, \, p = .14$$

This result—the result that researchers would actually obtain—seems to indicate that the groups are not significantly different. It would produce the inaccurate conclusion that the independent variable has no effect on the dependent variable. Temporary omniscience allows us to see the "true story" and to realize that this conclusion is driven (partially) by poor reliability.

Thus, researchers who ignore reliability risk drawing mistaken conclusions. Indeed, reliability is an important issue for all researchers—for those who study "individual differences" and those who do not think they study individual differences, for those who conduct experiments and those who conduct non-experimental research. To facilitate examination of reliability, the next section discusses the most common ways of estimating reliability.

Estimating reliability

Thus far, discussion has focussed on theoretical concepts such as true scores, measurement error, and true-score effect sizes. Indeed, it assumed temporary omniscience at several points, and it defined reliability in terms of unseen properties. This section shifts from theory to practice.

Because reliability is defined in terms of unseen properties researchers must estimate it—they cannot know the actual reliability of their scores. There are at least three methods of estimating reliability—alternate forms (i.e., parallel tests), internal consistency, and test–retest. Because researchers rarely use alternate forms, this section focusses on internal consistency and (to a lesser degree) test–retest (see Furr & Bacharach, 2008 for additional discussion of all three).

Internal consistency The most common methods of estimating reliability are based upon internal consistency. If a test includes multiple items and if a participant's score is computed by aggregating (i.e., summing or averaging) responses across items, then the score is called a composite score. Most scales are of this kind, with most scale scores being composite scores. Internal consistency methods are potentially useful for estimating the reliability of composite scores. There are several internal consistency approaches to reliability (e.g., split half, KR-20, coefficient alpha), primarily representing applicability to different response formats (i.e., binary items vs non-binary items) and applicability to data meeting different assumptions.

From this approach, two factors affect the reliability of scale scores. The first is the consistency among the "parts" of a scale. A multi-item scale can be seen as having multiple-parts—for example, each item can be considered a part of a test, or the scale can be divided into two sets of items, with each set being one "part" of the scale. However, a scale's parts are conceptualized, strong correlations among those parts raises the reliability of its scores. That is, if observed differences (among participants) on one part of the scale are consistent with observed differences on the other parts, then observed differences in participants' scores on the entire scale are fairly consistent with differences in their true scores. The second factor affecting reliability is scale length—a scale with many items is likely to have greater reliability than a scale with few items. This is due to the nature of measurement error.

The popularity of coefficient alpha (i.e., Cronbach's alpha) motivates particular attention. Alpha is an "item-level" internal consistency approach, using inter-item associations to estimate reliability of scale scores. Several statistical software packages provide two versions of alpha—raw and standardized. These versions are often similar, but they can·differ dramatically in some cases and they are relevant to different scale usages.

Raw alpha is a reliability estimate for composite scores based upon raw, unaltered responses. That is, if one wishes to sum or average item "raw" item responses, then raw alpha is an appropriate estimate of reliability. For example, imagine a 4-item scale with a 7-point Likert-type response format, with responses from five hypothetical participants (see Table 4.3). If these unaltered responses are summed or averaged to create composite scores, then the "raw alpha" estimate is appropriate.

In the first step of a two-step computational process, item-level and scale-level statistics are calculated. Specifically, the covariance between each pair of items is computed (i.e., all $s_{ii'}$ values, reflecting associations between variables), as is the variance of total observed scores $(s^2_{O_X})$. For the data in Table 4.3., $s^2_{O_X} = 17.20$ and the covariances are:

	Item 1	Item 2	Item 3	Item 4
Item 1		2.24	−0.12	1.52
Item 2	2.24		0.12	1.08
Item 3	−0.12	0.12		−0.04
Item 4	1.52	1.08	−0.04	

Table 4.3 Hypothetical data for internal consistency method of estimating reliability

Persons	Items 1	2	3	4	Total Score
1	7	6	4	6	23
2	4	5	5	6	20
3	2	1	4	4	11
4	3	4	5	3	15
5	3	5	4	4	16
Mean	3.8	4.2	4.4	4.6	17
Variance	2.96	2.96	0.24	1.44	17.2

These covariances reveal a potential problem—several values are near zero or negative. If the items are good measures of the same psychological variable, then they should all have positive covariances. Thus, the presence of small or negative covariances suggest that either: a) some items do not measure the same psychological variable as other items; or b) some items are affected heavily by measurement error (e.g., they are phrased ambiguously, leading participants to respond in ways that do not reflect their true scores).

The second step in computing raw alpha is to enter the summed covariances, the variance of composite scores, and the number of items (k) into:

$$\text{raw alpha} = \text{estimated } r_{xx} = \left(\frac{k}{k-1} \right) \left(\frac{\Sigma s_{ii'}}{s_x^2} \right)$$

For Table 4.3's data,

$$\text{raw alpha} = \text{estimated } r_{xx} = \left(\frac{4}{4-1} \right) \left(\frac{9.60}{17.20} \right) \qquad \text{(Equation 4.4)}$$

$$\text{raw alpha} = \text{estimated } r_{xx} = (1.33)(.56)$$

$$\text{raw alpha} = \text{estimated } r_{xx} = .74$$

Thus, the estimated reliability of the raw scores from the 4-item scale is .74. Note that this estimate is fairly high, despite the problems noted above (i.e., weak, even negative covariances). This good level of reliability is obtained because the problems are limited to item #3, which has the least amount of variability. Because the other three items are all strongly related to each other and because, as shown in Table 4.3, they have greater variability than does item #3 (which essentially weights their effects more strongly), the overall scale reliability is quite good. Many popular statistical software packages provide "raw alpha" reliability estimates—for example, SPSS's "Reliability Analysis" procedure labels this as "Cronbach's Alpha" (see Figure 4.5).

The "standardized alpha" provided by several statistical packages is appropriate if one standardizes responses to each item before aggregating across items. Researchers might standardize responses if items have dramatically-different

Reliability Statistics

Cronbach's Alpha	Cronbach's Alpha Based on Standardized Items	N of Items
.744	.658	4

Item Statistics

	Mean	Standard Deviation	N
Item1	3.8000	1.92354	5
Item2	4.2000	1.92354	5
Item3	4.4000	.54772	5
Item4	4.6000	1.34164	5

Item-Total Statistics

	Scale mean if Item Deleted	Scale Variance if Item Deleted	Corrected Item-Total Correlation	Squared Multiple Correlation	Cronbach's Alpha if Item Deleted
Item1	13.2000	8.700	.802	.767	.500
Item2	12.8000	9.200	.737	.641	.554
Item3	12.6000	21.300	−.020	.174	.852
Item4	12.4000	13.300	.654	.549	.632

Figure 4.5   Estimating reliability: results of reliability analysis

variabilities, in order to prevent composite scores from reflecting primarily the item(s) with greatest variability. This is not necessary in typical measurement contexts; however, it would be necessary if items were scaled on different metrics (e.g., some are on a 5-point scale and some are on a 7-point scale). Similarly, it would likely be appropriate when scores from different measures are combined to generate an aggregated measure (e.g., combining GPA and SAT scores to create a composite index of "academic ability"). In such cases, standardization is important and standardized alpha is appropriate.

Standardized alpha is again computed through a two-step procedure. For example, imagine that the items in Table 4.3 are to be standardized before aggregating. In the first step of estimating reliability of the composited standardized scores, correlations among all items are computed (all r_{ij} values), reflecting the degree to which differences among the participants' response to the items are consistent with each other:

Item pair	Correlation
1&2	$r_{12} = .76$
1&3	$r_{13} = -.13$
1&4	$r_{14} = .74$
2&3	$r_{23} = .14$
2&4	$r_{24} = .52$
3&4	$r_{34} = -.07$

In the second step, estimated reliability is obtained by entering the average inter-item correlation ($\bar{r}_{ii'}$) and the number of items (k) into:

$$\text{standardized alpha} = \text{estimated } r_{xx} = \frac{k\bar{r}_{ii'}}{1+(k-1)\bar{r}_{ii'}} \qquad \text{(Equation 4.5)}$$

$$\text{standardized alpha} = \text{estimated } r_{xx} = \frac{4(.32)}{1+(4-1).32}$$

$$\text{standardized alpha} = \text{estimated } r_{xx} = .65$$

This value is labeled "Cronbach's Alpha Based on Standardized Items" by SPSS (see Figure 4.5).

The estimated reliability of scale scores provides important information about the psychometric quality of those scores, indicating whether the scale should be improved. If estimated reliability is low (say below .70 or .80), then researchers who are constructing a scale should consider additional revisions and improvements to the scale (see Figure 2.1). If estimated reliability is acceptable, then researchers should examine the appropriate psychological interpretations of scale scores (i.e., validity, Chapter 5).

The accuracy of alpha (or any other method) as an estimate of reliability hinges on several psychometric assumptions. Fortunately, the assumptions underlying alpha are somewhat more liberal than those underlying the use of many other methods. See Chapter 8 and other sources (e.g., Feldt & Brennan, 1989) for more details.

Alpha is often described as a lower-bound estimate of reliability, but it can underestimate or overestimate reliability. Because internal consistency methods rely upon responses from a single measurement occasion, they do not account for measurement error affecting responses during the entire measurement occasion. Some sources of error (e.g., fatigue) might affect a participant's responses to all items during one measurement occasion, but might not affect his or her responses on another measurement occasion. By focussing on a single measurement occasion, internal consistency approaches might underestimate the totality of error affecting scale scores, thereby overestimating reliability.

An important point should be reiterated—alpha is not an index of unidimensionality. A scale having a large alpha value is not necessarily unidimensional. True, alpha is affected by internal consistency (e.g., the correlations among items), and strongly unidimensional scales should have good internal consistency. However, alpha is also affected by scale length—all else being equal, longer scales have greater alpha values than briefer scales. Thus, a high alpha value could mean either that the scale is unidimensional or that it is multidimensional (probably with correlated dimensions) but long. As discussed earlier, dimensionality should be examined through procedures such as factor analysis.

Test–retest   Although internal consistency approaches are the most common method of estimating reliability in psychological research, the test–retest approach is informative and may be the only viable strategy for some measures. As the label implies, this approach requires participants to complete the measure on two occasions.

There are several assumptions underlying the test–retest approach. The first is that there are no changes in the true score (psychological) differences among participants. A second assumption is that error variance of the first occasion is equal to error variance of the second. These assumptions imply that the two measurement occasions produce scores that are equally reliable. If these assumptions are valid, then the correlation between scores from the two measurement occasions is an estimate of reliability.

Although the second assumption might be fairly reasonable in many circumstances, the first is highly questionable for many important psychological characteristics. Specifically, in some test–retest examinations, participants' true scores might change between measurements. There are several factors affecting the likely validity of the stability assumption. First, some attributes are less stable than others. Transient or state-like characteristics are certainly less stable than trait-like characteristics, and thus test–retest estimates are inadvisable for measures of state-like attributes. A second factor related to the stability assumption is the length of the test–retest interval—longer intervals likely allow greater changes in true scores. In social/personality psychology, test–retest intervals of two to eight weeks seem common. A third factor related to the stability assumption is the developmental period at which the test–retest interval occurs. Psychological change/instability may be more likely during some periods in an individual's life (e.g., early childhood) than in others. Despite its limitations, the test–retest approach is often the only way to estimate reliability for single-item scales (which cannot be evaluated via internal consistency methods).

Reliability information for scale construction and improvement

As discussed earlier, estimated reliability is important psychometric information indicating whether a scale needs further attention and improvement; however, it provides little guidance regarding specific strategies for making improvements. There are several strategies for improving reliability, and guidance is revealed through several important item-level statistics.

Lengthen the scale   According to CTT, reliability can be improved by adding good items to a scale. Recall that CTT assumes that measurement error is random—if a participant's response to one item is artificially high (e.g., she mistakenly marks 7 for "strongly agree" rather than 6 for "agree"), then some of her responses to other items might be artificially low. Across a sufficient number of items, artificial deflation should balance out artificial inflation—ultimately producing an observed score closely matching the participant's true score. Longer scales provide greater opportunity for error to balance out.

In fact, researchers can forecast the likely reliability of a revised scale—e.g., a scale having more (or perhaps fewer, for reasons of efficiency) items than an original scale. For example, a researcher considers adding two items to the 4-item scale reflected in Table 4.3 (representing a revised scale 1.5 times as long as the original). The following version of the Spearman–Brown Prophecy formula can be used to forecast the reliability of a revised scale $(r_{XX\text{-}revised})$:

$$r_{XX-revised} \quad \frac{f r_{XX-original}}{1+(f-1)r_{xx-original}} \qquad \text{(Equation 4.6)}$$

Where $r_{XX\text{-}original}$ is the estimated reliability of the original scale, and f is the factor to which the scale is lengthened or shortened. For the potential 6-item revised scale,

$$r_{XX-revised} = \frac{1.5(.74)}{1+(1.5-1).74}$$

$$r_{XX-revised} = .81$$

Thus, assuming that the scale is lengthened to a factor of 1.5 by adding items psychometrically equivalent to existing items, the revised scale should have a reliability of .81.

Such forecasts can guide scale construction by identifying scale-lengths that could meet specified levels of reliability. For example, a researcher could enter several potential "lengthening factor" values, finding the length that would produce scale scores with $r_{XX} = .80$. Of course, after a scale is revised, new data should be collected and new analyses should be conducted to obtain solid estimates of psychometric quality.

Improve inter-item correlations   The second way of improving reliability is to increase the correlations among a scale's items—that is, to enhance the scale's internal consistency. The previous chapter discussed the importance of items that are written clearly and that are relevant to the intended psychological variable. When people respond to such items, their responses should exhibit good psychometric qualities, which in turn should enhance the internal consistency among the items, which should improve reliability. Psychometric analysis can reveal poor items that should be rewritten or eliminated. Indeed, popular statistical software packages provide information regarding the psychometric quality of individual items—as represented by output in Figure 4.5.

Perhaps the most fundamental statistical aspect of an item's quality is its variability. Due to restricted range, items with little variability are unlikely to correlate well with other items. Thus, they are candidates for exclusion or revision. As shown in Table 4.3 and Figure 4.5, item 3 (from the four-item hypothetical scale) has lower variability than do other items. This suggests that item 3 might warrant revision or elimination.

A second fundamental statistical aspect of an item's quality is its association with the other items in its scale. This is reflected in several ways, and an item having weak associations with other items is a candidate for revision or elimination. One way of examining this is, of course, the item's correlations with other items. The correlations among the hypothetical items in Table 4.4 were presented earlier, and they revealed that item 3 has noticeably weak correlations with the other items—in fact, it is somewhat negatively correlated with items 1 and 4. Thus, the differences in participants' responses to item 3 are inconsistent with the differences in their responses to the other items. A second useful piece of information is an item's item-total correlation, or corrected item-total correlation as shown in Figure 4.5. A corrected item-total correlation is the correlation between an item and a composite of all other items, reflecting the degree to which it is consistent with the other items as a whole. Figure 4.5 reveals a very low item-total correlation for item 3, reaffirming the message from its weak pairwise associations. A third useful piece of information is an item's squared multiple correlation. This is an R^2 value reflecting the proportion of variance in an item that is explained by the other items. Again, it represents the degree to which the item is associated with the other items as a whole, and once again Figure 4.5 suggests that item 3 is relatively poor.

A third and related aspect is an item's impact on the overall reliability of scale scores. Figure 4.5 presents "alpha if deleted" values, providing direct insight into the potential value of eliminating each item. An item's "alpha if deleted" value reflects the estimated reliability of a scale that includes all items except for that item. Thus, Figure 4.5 suggests that eliminating item 3 would produce a three-item scale having an estimated reliability of .85. This value is noticeably larger than the estimated reliability of .74 for the entire four-item scale. This information clearly indicates that item 3 should be revised or eliminated.

This example demonstrates that the "longer scales are better" rule is not always true—in this case, a three-item scale would have better reliability than the four-item scale. This can arise if the longer scale includes bad items—items that are inconsistent with the other items on the scale. Thus, the "longer scales are better" rule is best interpreted as "longer scales are better, all else being equal." In Table 4.3, all else is *not* equal, because the longer scale has poorer internal consistency than does the three-item scale that excludes item 3. Thus, the greater length of the four-item scale does not offset its weaker internal consistency.

Inter-rater reliability

Many researchers rely upon people as instruments of measurement, asking raters to observe and rate psychological phenomena such as behavior or personality. For example, researchers might study pro-social behavior expressed during dyadic interactions. For this work, researchers might video-record participants engaged in a dyadic task, and then ask raters to watch those videotapes and rate the participants' pro-social behavior. In such work, researchers should (and usually do) obtain ratings from multiple raters; thus, reliability hinges on the consistency or agreement among the raters. If raters are consistent with each other, then reliability is assumed to be high. If, however, raters are inconsistent (or disagree), then reliability is low and the ratings are of questionable quality.

Thus, inter-rater reliability (or agreement) is an important issue for many researchers, and several methods are used to gauge it. The most familiar methods are Cohen's kappa (in various forms), weighted kappa, coefficient alpha, intra-class correlations, and Generalizability Theory. One's choice of method hinges on several considerations: a) the number of raters; b) the nature of the rating scale itself (i.e., are rating dichotomous or are there more than two response options for each construct being measured?); c) the level of measurement (i.e., nominal, ordinal, etc.); d) way in which raters are assigned to participants; and e) the intended use of the rating data (i.e., as "absolute" values or as reflecting the "relative" differences among participants).

Cohen's kappa and several variants are popular choices for examinations of inter-rater agreement (e.g., Kraemer et al., 2002). The simplest form of kappa is designed for two raters and two response options (e.g., two raters judging whether participants exhibited a specific behavior, with analyses conducted for each behavior that is measured). More advanced forms of kappa (e.g., Fleiss's kappa) can accommodate more than two raters and/or more than two response options (e.g., three raters judging which of four behaviors each participant exhibited). However, some of these cannot accommodate an ordinal/interval level of measurement, treating all "disagreements" equally. This is clearly inappropriate for data in which raters use ordinal/interval scales to rate behaviors (or whatever the phenomenon is) in terms of degree (e.g., in terms of Likert-type ratings of a behavior's intensity or frequency). In such cases, kappa treats psychologically-minor disagreements (e.g., one rater rates a participant as being "very highly" talkative and another rates him/her as "highly" talkative) just like major disagreements (e.g., one rater rates a participant as "very highly" talkative and another rates him/her as "not at all" talkative). For such ordinal/interval ratings, researchers might use a weighted kappa, in which some disagreements are weighted more strongly than others. Thus, there are many forms of kappa, providing flexibility in terms of evaluating inter-rater agreement. Unfortunately, missing data are not well-accommodated by the basic variants of kappa.

Fortunately, intraclass correlations (ICCs) are another familiar approach to inter-rater reliability, offering great flexibility in important ways (including handling missing data). Particularly for ratings made on ordinal/interval scales, ICCs are a strong method for evaluating inter-rater reliability. Indeed, they offer flexibility in terms of the number of raters, the number of participants, the number of response options, the ability to handle missing data, and the intended use of rating data. Interestingly, coefficient alpha is one version of an ICC that is appropriate as in index of inter-rater reliability. A full discussion of ICCs is beyond the scope of the current chapter, but details are available in other sources (e.g., Shrout & Fleiss, 1979). Moreover, ICCs can be integrated within the framework of Generalizability Theory, which is discussed in Chapter 9. As discussed and illustrated in that chapter, ICCs and Generalizability Theory more generally are highly adaptable and useful techniques for evaluating reliability—including interrater reliability.

Summary

This chapter introduced two fundamental facets of psychometric quality. Dimensionality refers to the nature and number of psychological dimensions underlying responses to a scale's items. This affects the scoring and interpretation of a scale, and it has implications for subsequent psychometric evaluations. Reliability refers to the precision with which scale scores reflect the psychological variable affecting the participants' responses. This has direct implications for the magnitude of experimental effects produced by the scale and, consequently, for the statistical significance of those effects. Indeed, scale construction and use that proceeds without attention to dimensionality and reliability may produce scores with no clear psychological meaning and may contribute to inaccurate psychological conclusions.

Notes

1 Cohen's $d = \dfrac{\bar{X}_1 - \bar{X}_2}{s_{pooled}}$, where $s_{pooled} = \sqrt{\dfrac{(n_1)s_1^2 + (n_2)s_2^2}{n_1 + n_2}}$

2 There are several versions of the Spearman–Brown Prophecy formula. For example, another version bases its forecast on the average inter-item correlation of the original scale and the number of items in the potential revised scale.

5

Evaluating Psychometric Properties: Validity

Dimensionality and reliability are important facets of a scale's psychometric properties and quality, but validity is the most crucial facet. Even if dimensionality and reliability of scale scores are clear and robust, poor validity compromises a scale's psychological utility. This chapter defines validity, addresses its importance for scale construction and use, and presents the types of evidence to consider when gauging validity.

This discussion reflects a contemporary perspective that differs from the familiar "tripartite" perspective on validity. Whereas the traditional perspective differentiates three types of validity (i.e., content, criterion, and construct), the contemporary perspective emphasizes construct validity as the central issue. From this perspective, content validity and criterion validity are types of evidence informing the core concept of construct validity. Other good sources provide detailed discussions of this perspective (e.g., Messick, 1989; Zumbo, 2007).

Meaning of Validity

From the contemporary perspective, validity is "the degree to which evidence and theory support the interpretations of test scores entailed by the proposed uses" of a scale (AERA et al., 1999, p. 9). Thus, the evaluation of validity is "an ongoing process wherein one provides evidence to support the appropriateness, meaningfulness and usefulness of the specific inferences made from scores about individuals from a given sample and in a given context" (Zumbo, 2007, p. 48). This view focusses on understanding the psychological construct affecting responses to the scale, underscoring construct validity as the heart of measurement validity.

These definitions have several important implications:

1 *Validity concerns the interpretation of scale scores, not scales themselves.* That is, it concerns the psychological inferences drawn from scale scores. Relatedly, validity is linked to the "proposed uses" of scale scores, which is perhaps a more important issue in applied testing than in research (e.g., should SAT scores be used in admissions

processes, should the MMPI be used for hiring decisions?). In these ways, psychological scales are like tools in any profession—a tool can be useful for some purposes but not others. Thus, a psychological scale can produce scores that are validly interpreted and used in some ways but not in others.

2   *Validity is a matter of degree, it is not "all-or-none."* Validity should be weighed in terms of strong versus weak evidence, and a scale should be used with confidence only if there is convincing evidence of its appropriate interpretation and use.

3   *Validity requires evidence and theory.* For researchers and readers to use and interpret a scale confidently, good empirical evidence must support its psychological meaning and utility.

4   *The "appropriateness, meaningfulness, and usefulness" of scale scores is contextually constrained.* The psychological meaning of a scale's scores in one context or within one population might differ from their meaning as derived from a different context or within a different population. Particularly for groups and contexts differing dramatically from the ones within (and for) which a scale was originally constructed and evaluated, new empirical evidence of the scale's psychological meaning is required.

5   *There is no single quantitative value that reflects validity.* Validation involves many considerations—some theoretical, some empirical, and some involving social or even political issues. There is no single number or statistical test capturing the complexity and wide-ranging nature of validity.

Importance of Validity

Validity's importance is straightforward—accurate description, prediction, and explanation of psychological phenomena depend upon researchers' ability to manipulate or measure important variables Thus, researchers and readers must be confident that the proposed (perhaps implicit) interpretations of scale scores are, in fact, warranted and accurate. Indeed, "without validation, any inferences made from a measure are potentially meaningless, inappropriate and of limited usefulness" (Zumbo, 2007, p. 48).

Evaluating Validity

The American Education Research Association (AERA), the American Psychological Association (APA), and the National Council on Measurement in Education (NCME) delineated five types of evidence relevant to validity. As shown in Figure 5.1, construct validity is the heart of the matter, with evidence reflected in a scale's content, its internal structure, the psychological process used in responding to the scale, the consequences of its use, and the association among its scores and other variables.

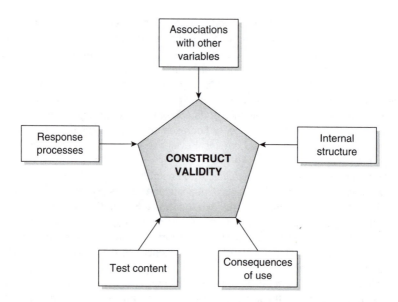

Figure 5.1   A contemporary perspective of types of information relevant to test validity

Scale content

One form of validity evidence is the match between actual scale content and the content that *should be* in the scale. As reflected in the first two steps of the scale construction process (Figure 2.1), if scale scores are to be interpreted in terms of a particular psychological phenomenon, then its content must reflect important facets of that phenomenon—no more, no less.

Researchers should be alert to two sources of content *in*validity. The first is construct-irrelevant content—content that is irrelevant to the construct for which the scale is to be interpreted (e.g., a supposed measure of global self-esteem includes some items reflecting social skill). The second is construct-underrepresentation, which occurs when a scale omits content relevant to the intended construct (e.g., a supposed measure of global self-esteem includes items reflecting only academic self-esteem). Either problem compromises researchers' ability to interpret a scale in terms of the intended construct.

Presumably, well-guided scale construction produces scales with good "content validity." Indeed, careful articulation of the psychological construct, alongside thoughtful and critical evaluation (and re-evaluation) of item content, should produce scales with content that accurately reflects their intended constructs. Content validity can be evaluated by people with a solid understanding of the relevant psychological variable—people who can detect construct-irrelevant content and construct underrepresentation. Very strong evidence of content validity would be obtained through scrutiny and approval by experts who were not personally involved in item writing. Such evidence provides an independent source of evaluation, going beyond a researcher's opinions about a scale that he or she has created.

Face validity is not content validity. Again, content validity is the degree to which a scale truly reflects its intended construct—no more, no less. In contrast, face validity is the degree to which a measure appears related to a specific construct, as perceived by those who might not be knowledgeable about the construct. Non-experts might not be able to critically and thoroughly evaluate the theoretical and empirical meaning of the scale's intended psychological construct. Thus, content validity, but not face validity, is an important form of evidence in the overall evaluation of construct validity. Unfortunately, researchers sometimes seem to rely upon face validity and assume that a scale's validity is self-evident.

Internal structure

A second validity issue concerns a scale's internal structure or dimensionality. Specifically, validity depends partially upon the match between the *actual* internal structure of a scale and the structure that the scale *should* possess. If a scale is to be interpreted as a measure of a particular construct, then its actual structure should match the construct's theoretically-based structure. For example, a scale intended to reflect a single construct should have a clear unidimensional structure, but a scale intended to reflect a multi-dimensional construct should have a corresponding multidimensional structure.

As discussed in Chapter 4, exploratory factor analysis (EFA) is often used to evaluate a scale's dimensionality. EFA is indeed useful, but researchers must make somewhat subjective judgments regarding the match between a scale's internal structure and the hypothesized structure of the relevant construct. Thus, Chapter 8 presents Confirmatory Factor Analysis (CFA), which is a tool for formally-evaluating the "fit" between a hypothesized structure and a scale's actual structure. With increasing availability of CFA-capable software, researchers have greater opportunity to evaluate effectively the internal structure facet of validity.

Response processes

A third facet of validity is the match between the psychological processes that *actually* affect responses and the processes that *should* affect those responses (based on the scale's intended meaning). This perspective is promoted perhaps most strongly by Borsboom et al. (2004), who suggest that the sole issue in test validity is whether test responses are affected by the construct that the test is intended to measure. That is, a test is a valid measure of a construct only if the intended construct truly influences respondents' performance on the scale. They suggest that "the primary objective of validation research is ... to offer a theoretical explanation of the processes that lead up to the measurement outcome" (p. 1067).

Borsboom et al. criticize much of psychology for failing to attend to this facet of validity. Moreover, they suggest that attention must begin with clear theories of the psychological processes underlying participants' responses. Relatedly, Embretson (1983) offers mathematical models to address "construct representation," which concerns the "theoretical mechanisms that underlie" responses to a psychological measure (p. 180). These models expand upon Item Response Theory (see Chapter 10).

Consequences of scale use   Perhaps the most controversial element of the contemporary view of validity is the suggestion that the consequences of scale use are a facet of validity. While some researchers agree that test developers, users, and evaluators have a responsibility to examine the application of tests or scales, others wonder about the potential role of social, political, and personal values in the scientific process of scale validation. Indeed, some argue that "consequential validity is a dangerous intrusion of politics into science" (Lees-Haley, 1996, p. 982).

Although "consequential validity" might be most salient in applied contexts, it reminds us that theoretical assumptions and choices are partially shaped by value judgments. Even the labels applied to theoretical concepts or scales are partially shaped by values. Moreover, are such choices shaped by socially-relevant findings, such as gender differences or ethnic differences? Attention to consequential validity requires that such effects and issues should be acknowledged and evaluated.

Associations with other variables

The fifth—and perhaps most familiar—form of validity concerns the association between scale scores and measures (or manipulations) of other psychological variables. Whether framed in terms of convergent validity, discriminant validity, predictive validity, or concurrent validity, "associative" evidence places scales in the context of other psychological variables. By doing so, it provides insight into the construct affecting scale scores. Moreover, a construct's theoretical basis implies a network of similar and dissimilar psychological variables. That is, the theoretical definition of a variable implies a pattern of associations—which variables are closely connected, which are more distal, and which (perhaps implicitly) are unrelated to the construct supposedly being measured.

Validity, then, hinges on the match between a scale's *actual* associations with other measures and the associations that the test *should have* with the other measures. If the pattern of actual associations matches the pattern implied by the theoretical definition of the intended construct, then researchers and readers gain confidence that scale scores can be interpreted in terms of that construct. However, if the patterns do *not* match, then researchers and readers should hesitate to interpret scale scores in terms of the intended construct.

When evaluating this associative facet of validity, researchers and readers should consider both convergent and discriminant evidence. Convergent evidence is the degree to which scale scores are associated with measures or manipulations of related constructs. For example, self-report scores on a self-esteem scale should be positively correlated with informant-reports of self-esteem (a different measure of the same construct) and they should be negatively correlated with self-report scores on a measure of depressive affect (a construct that is theorized to be negatively associated with self-esteem). Discriminant evidence is obtained when scale scores are *not* associated with measures or manipulations of *un*related constructs. For example, self-report scores on a self-esteem scale should be weakly- or uncorrelated with self-reported creativity or with intelligence, assuming that neither is theoretically linked to self-esteem.

The importance of convergent evidence is probably obvious, but the importance of discriminant evidence is perhaps under-appreciated. If researchers and readers wish to interpret scale scores in terms of a specific construct, then there must be evidence that scores truly reflect that construct *and only that construct*. To borrow an example (Furr & Bacharach, 2008), consider a study of the association between self-esteem and academic ability. Researchers ask students to complete a supposed self-esteem scale, they obtain students' standardized achievement test scores, they discover a correlation of .40 between scale scores and achievement scores, and they conclude that students who have relatively high self-esteem tend to perform relatively well in school. Such a conclusion might have important practical and theoretical implications; however, before accepting this conclusion, researchers and readers should consider (among other things) discriminant evidence regarding the supposed self-esteem scale. If scale scores are highly correlated with measures of intelligence (and if intelligence is not hypothesized to be linked to self-esteem), then the scale lacks clear discriminant validity and is at least partially a measure of intelligence. Thus, the supposed association between self-esteem and academic achievement might be more accurately interpreted as indicating that students who have relatively high intelligence tend to perform relatively well in school. Indeed, self-esteem might actually be unrelated to academic performance, but the use of a scale with poor discriminant validity compromises the psychological conclusions.

Thus, researchers should consider convergent *and* discriminant evidence carefully when interpreting scale scores. Failure to consider either type of evidence compromises the argument that scale scores reflect a specific construct and only that construct, and this in turn compromises the accuracy of psychological conclusion based upon those scale scores. Many important considerations arise when evaluating convergent and discriminant evidence, and the next section discusses these key considerations.

Focus on "Associative" Validity Evidence

Associative validity evidence is perhaps the most empirically-challenging facet of validity. This section introduces several ways of evaluating convergent and discriminant evidence, and it discusses relevant methodological issues. Additional detail is available in Furr and Bacharach (2008).

Methods of evaluating convergent and discriminant evidence

Focussed associations   Although some scales are intended to measure constructs with implications across many areas of behavior, cognition, or affect, others have strong relevance for only a few specific outcomes. For such "narrow-focus" tests or scales, convergent and discriminant evidence focusses on the associations between test/scale scores on only the variables most relevant to the test's purpose. For example, the SAT Reasoning test is intended to assess "the critical thinking skills students need for academic success in college" (College Board, nd), which has led researchers to focus on associations between SAT scores and measures of collegiate academic performance (i.e., college GPA). Such highly-focussed associations have all-or-none implications for convergent validity evidence—empirical confirmation of the predicted associations provides strong evidence, but disconfirmation casts serious doubt on validity.

Sets of associations   As mentioned earlier, the conceptual foundation of a construct implies a pattern or network of associations with other variables. Such networks likely include some variables with strong associations to the construct of interest and some variables with weaker associations to that construct. In these cases, associative evidence must be examined across a range of criterion variables. Indeed, researchers often compute correlations between a scale of interest and measures of many criterion variables, then "eyeball" the correlations to judge whether they match what is expected on the basis of the construct's hypothesized pattern of associations. This approach is common and potentially useful, but it provides no formalized evaluation of the overall hypothesized pattern of associations. The remaining two approaches provide more formalized or organized evaluations.

Multitrait-multimethod matrices   Analysis of multitrait-multimethod matrices (MTMM) has a long history (Campbell & Fiske, 1959), and it organizes the examination of associative evidence in a way that goes beyond the typical "set of associations" approach. In an MTMM study, researchers examine associations among several psychological variables, each being measured through several methods. For example, researchers constructing a new self-report scale of Locus of Control might measure participants on four psychological constructs (e.g., Locus of Control, Need for Cognition, Self-esteem, and Social Skill) by using three methods to measure each construct (e.g., self-report, reports by participants' close acquaintances, and ratings by trained interviewers). They then compute correlations among all measures of all constructs, creating a "multitrait-multimethod" correlation matrix. As defined in Table 5.1, MTMM matrices include four types of correlations.

Table 5.1   MTMM framework

Association between the two constructs		Method used to measure the two constructs	
		Different methods	Same methods
Different constructs (not associated)	**Label**	Heterotrait–Heteromethod correlations	Heterotrait–Monomethod correlations
	Example	Self-report measure of Locus of Control correlated with informant-report measure of Social Skill	Self-report measure of Locus of Control correlated with self-report measure of Social Skill
	Sources of variance	Non-shared trait variance & Non-shared method variance	Non-shared trait variance & Shared method variance
	Expected correlation	Weakest	Moderate
Same (or similar) constructs (associated)	**Label**	Monotrait–Heteromethod correlations	Monotrait–Monomethod correlations
	Example	Self-report measure of Locus of Control correlated with informant-report measure of Locus of Control	Self-report measure of Locus of Control correlated with self-report measure of Locus of Control (i.e., reliability)
	Sources of variance	Shared trait variance & Non-shared method variance	Shared trait variance & Shared method variance
	Expected correlation	Strong	Strongest

Based upon this structure, MTMM analysis provides guidelines for evaluating associative evidence (see Table 5.1). For example, heterotrait–heteromethod correlations should be relatively weak because the correlated variables share neither a common construct nor a common method. That is, a good self-report measure of Locus of Control should be correlated only weakly (if at all) with an acquaintance-report measure of Social Skill. In contrast, monotrait–heteromethod correlations should be somewhat stronger, because the correlated variables share a common construct (though not a common method). A good self-report measure of Locus of Control should be moderately or strongly correlated with good acquaintance-reports of Locus of Control. If the observed pattern of correlations in the MTMM matrix fits the pattern of predicted associations outlined in Table 5.1, then researchers have obtained good associative evidence.

Researchers have developed sophisticated analytic strategies for MTMM data. Despite this statistical attention, the MTMM approach does not seem to be used frequently in validational "practice." However, it has been important in the understanding and analysis of convergent and discriminant validity evidence, and it is used to address other interesting psychological questions.

Quantifying construct validity   The previously-discussed approaches to evaluating associative evidence often rely upon researchers' subjective judgments of correlations. Even from an MTMM approach, researchers make somewhat subjective decisions about the degree to which the pattern of correlations matches the pattern predicted on the basis of the MTMM framework (e.g., is the monotrait–heteromethod correlation sufficiently greater than the heterotrait–heteromethod correlations?).

In contrast, the "Quantifying Construct Validity" (QCV) procedure provides an objective quantitative estimate of the support provided by the overall pattern of associative evidence (Westen & Rosenthal, 2003). This procedure quantifies the "fit" between: a) a pattern of predicted convergent and discriminant correlations; and b) the pattern of correlations that are actually obtained.

QCV produces two kinds of results. First, it produces effect sizes representing the *degree of fit* between the actual pattern of correlations and the predicted pattern of correlations. A full discussion of these effect sizes is beyond the scope of this volume, but they are correlational values. Thus, large positive effect sizes (i.e., values approaching +1) indicate that the actual pattern of associative correlations closely matches the pattern implied by the construct's conceptual basis. QCV's second kind of result is a significance test indicating whether the fit between actual and predicted correlations is likely to have occurred by chance. Validity is supported by large effect sizes that are statistically significant.

The novel quality of QCV is that it formalizes the evaluation of associative evidence in terms of hypothesis evaluation. As such, it requires researchers to articulate specific hypotheses about the predicted pattern of validity correlations. They must think carefully about the criterion measures, forming clear predictions for each in terms of a correlation with the scale of interest. In addition, it summarizes the overall degree of support for the pattern of hypotheses. Although the procedure is not perfect, it is a potentially-important advance over methods relying upon subjective evaluations of the fit between predicted and actual patterns of correlations.

Factors affecting validity coefficients

All four of these strategies rely on the size of "validity coefficients" representing associations between a scale and criterion variables. When interpreting this evidence, researchers should consider several factors affecting the magnitude of validity coefficients. The following discussion focusses on correlations, but these factors affect any statistic reflecting associations between variables or differences between groups.

Association between constructs   The correlation between two measures is affected by the "true" association between the constructs reflected in those measures. If constructs are strongly positively associated with each other, then measures of those constructs will likely be robustly positively correlated. This is often the primary consideration for researchers forming hypotheses about one or more validity coefficients when evaluating a scale—which constructs are most strongly and weakly associated with the construct supposedly measured by the scale?

Measurement error and reliability As discussed in Chapter 4, Classical Test Theory states that measurement error and reliability directly affect a scale's associations with other variables. Specifically, measurement error reduces, or attenuates, the association between variables. Consequently, measurement error attenuates validity coefficients.

Therefore, when evaluating validity coefficients, researchers should consider the reliability of the focal scale and of the criterion variable(s). If either is poor, then validity coefficients are likely to be weak. Thus, even if the scale of interest has good psychometric quality, poor validity correlations will be obtained when criterion variables have poor reliability.

Restricted range Validity coefficients reflect associations between two variables, and the apparent association is affected by the range of scores obtained for either or both variables. If the range of scores in either variable is artificially limited or restricted, then the apparent association between variables can be artificially weak.

A familiar example is the apparent association between SAT scores and Academic Performance. Much of the associative evidence for the SAT hinges on correlations between SAT scores and Academic Performance as reflected by College GPA, but the apparent size of this association is reduced by range restriction in both variables. Students earning low SAT scores might not be admitted to colleges, excluding many "low SAT scorers" from contributing to analysis of the association between SAT scores and Academic Performance. Thus, the apparent size of this association might be obtained through samples that are restricted to people having SAT scores high enough to merit admission. The association between SAT scores and College GPA within such restricted samples likely underestimates the true association between SAT scores and the capacity for academic performance in college.

Thus, researchers should be aware that restricted range can reduce the size of correlations in validity studies. Apparently-low validity coefficients might underestimate the true association between a scale and criterion variables.

Skew and relative proportions A somewhat under-appreciated fact is that skew in a variable's distribution can affect the magnitude of correlations based upon that variable. All else being equal, correlations between a skewed distribution and a non-skewed distribution (or between distributions skewed in different ways) will be smaller than correlations between two non-skewed distributions (or between two distributions skewed in the same way).

This effect is perhaps clearest for correlations between a dichotomous variable and a continuous variable (i.e., point–biserial correlations, r_{pb}). The size of these correlations is affected by the relative proportions of participants in the groups defining the dichotomous variable:

$$|r_{PB}| = \frac{\sqrt{p_1 p_2} \left| \overline{C}_2 - \overline{C}_1 \right|}{s_C}$$

(Equation 5.1)

where p_1 and p_2 are the proportions of participants in group 1 and in group 2 respectively, $\overline{C}_1$ and $\overline{C}_2$ are the groups' means on the continuous variable, and s_C is the standard deviation of the continuous variable across the entire sample.[1]

For example, in a sample with a total standard deviation of 6.5 on a scale and with two equally-sized groups having scale means of 10 and 15, the correlation (between group membership and the continuous variable) is:

$$|r_{PB}| = \frac{\sqrt{.50 \times .50} \left| 10 - 15 \right|}{6.5} = .38$$

However, if group membership was extremely skewed so that there were ten times as many people in group 1 than in group 2, the correlation is reduced substantially:

$$|r_{PB}| = \frac{\sqrt{.909 \times .091} \left| 10 - 15 \right|}{6.5} = .22$$

Thus, as shown in Figure 5.2, for a given pair of means and a given standard deviation, the point–biserial correlation is largest when groups are equally sized. If groups have differing numbers of participants (as the proportion of participants in the two groups becomes widely divergent), then the correlation is reduced.

In sum, a subtle factor potentially affecting some validity coefficients is the skew in a variable, or analogously, the relative sizes of experimental groups. This issue should be considered when interpreting validity coefficients—an extremely-skewed variable or highly-divergent group sizes produce lower correlations than less-skewed variables or equally-sized groups.

Method variance   The apparent association between variables can be affected by similarity or dissimilarity in the methods used to measure them. In fact, a key facet of MTMM's logic is that associations are likely to be larger when variables are measured via the same/similar method than when measured via different methods. For example, the apparent association between self-esteem and intelligence is likely to be larger when both are measured via self-report than when self-esteem is measured via self-report and intelligence is measured via a traditional IQ test. Thus, when evaluating validity coefficients, researchers should be more

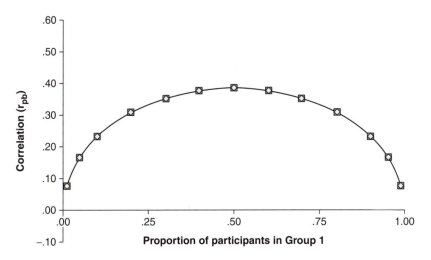

Figure 5.2   The effect of relative proportions of group sizes on point-biserial correlations

impressed by convergent evidence arising from correlations between different methods of assessment than by evidence from a single method.

Time   Researchers sometimes evaluate convergent evidence by examining associations between a scale completed at one point in time and criterion variables measured at a later time. All else being equal, associations between measures from different points in time (i.e., predictive validity correlations) are likely to be smaller than associations between measures from a single point in time (i.e., concurrent validity correlations). Correspondingly, longer periods between two points in time will likely produce smaller predictive validity correlations than will shorter periods.

Predictions of single events   The magnitude of a validity coefficient hinges partially upon the specificity of the criterion variable—that is, whether the criterion reflects a single event or an aggregation/accumulation of events. Single events or outcomes (e.g., a grade in a single class) are generally less predictable than are aggregations of events or accumulations of observations (e.g., cumulative GPA). This issue should be considered, particularly for apparently-weak validity coefficients based upon single-event criteria. For example, a small correlation between SAT scores and grades from a single class might not be a reasonable reflection of the SAT's true predictive validity.

Interpreting a validity coefficient

Researchers and readers evaluate the magnitude of validity coefficients—are they large enough to provide convincing convergent evidence, or are they small enough to provide clear discriminant evidence? The interpretation of an effect's magnitude is rather subjective—one person's "large correlation" or "robust difference" can appear small or weak to another person. Researchers and readers should consider several issues when interpreting the size and implications of validity coefficients.

Squared correlations and "variance explained" A common practice in psychological research is to interpret squared correlations as the proportion of variance in one variable that is explained or "accounted for" by another. This practice has several problems and should be done carefully. First, in some cases, the correlation itself, not the squared correlation, is interpretable as the proportion of variation explained (Ozer, 1985). Second, some experts argue that variance (based upon *squared* deviations from a mean) itself is on a non-intuitive metric, making "proportion of variance explained" a non-intuitive and non-useful concept. Third, some researchers argue that squaring a correlation makes the association between two variables seem too small—for example, a finding that the SAT explains "only" 22 percent of the variance in college GPA has led some people to conclude that the SAT is useless. Such interpretations are seriously misguided, which leads to the next issue.

Illustrative practical implications The strength of a validity coefficient can be framed in terms of practical implications, and there are several relevant procedures. Consider the Binomial Effect Size Display (BESD Rosenthal et al., 1982), which is usually formatted in terms of outcomes for a hypothetical group of 200 people—100 of whom have high scores on a variable and 100 of whom have low scores. For example, to reflect the association between SAT and college GPA, the BESD articulates the number of high SAT-scorers and low SAT-scorers who are likely to earn high or low College GPAs. Table 5.2 presents a BESD for this example, with values determined by:

$$\text{Cells A\&C} = 50 + 100\left(\frac{r}{2}\right)$$

$$\text{Cells B\&D} = 50 - 100\left(\frac{r}{2}\right)$$

Table 5.2   BESD example based upon r = .46

SAT score	College GPA	
	Low	High
Low	A	B
	73	27
High	C	D
	27	73

where r is the validity correlation between scale and criterion. If SAT scores are correlated with College GPA at r = .46 (i.e., from $R^2 = .22$), then 73 people (out of 100) with low SAT scores will likely earn relatively low GPAs and 73 people (out of 100) with relatively high SAT scores will likely earn relatively high GPAs:

$$\text{Cells A and C} = 50 + 100\left(\frac{.46}{2}\right)$$

$$\text{Cells A and C} = 73$$

Thus, a finding that SAT scores account for "only" 22 percent of the variance in college GPA roughly means that decisions informed by the SAT will be accurate (in terms of predicting who earns relatively high or low GPAs) 73 percent of the time and wrong only 27 percent of the time. This is not perfect, but it is quite good considering the multi-determination of the criterion, and it certainly does not support the conclusion that the SAT is useless or invalid as a predictor of College GPA. Although the BESD has been criticized, it and similar procedures provide practical interpretive contexts for validity coefficients.

Guidelines or norms for a field   The norms for an area of research or application provide another context for evaluating validity coefficients. Different areas of science have different norms for the associations typically found, and these norms should be considered when interpreting validity coefficients. For example, Cohen provided guidelines of .10, .30, and .50 as being small, medium, and large correlations in psychology (though these guidelines are problematic). Even within psychology, different disciplines might have different expectations for effect sizes. Thus, interpretations of validity coefficients, as with any index of association, need to be done with regard to a particular field. For example, in social psychology, Funder and Ozer (1983) examined several widely-cited and important effects (e.g., the effect of authority's proximity on obedience), finding an average correlational effect size slightly below .40. This is similar to the often-cited .30 "personality coefficient."

Statistical significance   Statistical significance plays an important role in psychological research, including validity evaluation. Thus, researchers and readers will likely consider whether a validity coefficient is statistically significant. Researchers expect significant effects when evaluating convergent validity evidence, but they generally expect non-significance when evaluating discriminant evidence.

Evaluation of a coefficient's statistical significance should be informed by consideration of the factors affecting significance. First is the coefficient's size—all else being equal, larger coefficients are more likely to be significant than are small coefficients. A second factor is the study's size, primarily in terms of sample size—all else being equal, larger samples increase the likelihood that validity coefficients will be significant. A third factor is the probability level used to determine significance (usually $\alpha = .05$).

Such issues should be considered when interpreting convergent and discriminant validity evidence. In studies based upon very large samples, weak validity coefficients might be statistically significant. That is, a significant validity coefficient might, in actuality, be weak—thereby providing weak convergent evidence or reasonable discriminant evidence. Moreover, in studies based upon small samples, strong validity coefficients might be non-significant. Thus, a non-significant validity coefficient might, in actuality, be strong—thereby providing better convergent evidence than non-significance would suggest, or it might be evidence of poor discriminant validity.

Summary

This chapter discussed validity as the accuracy with which scale scores are interpreted. If empirical evidence indicates that scores reflect a particular construct, then researchers and readers should have confidence in psychological conclusions drawn from those scores. This perspective on validity highlights five types of evidence bearing on construct validity, and this chapter addressed numerous issues to be considered when interpreting validity evidence.

Note

1 Note that the direction, but not the size, of r_{PB} depends on which group is designated 1 and which is designated 2.

6

Threats to Psychometric Quality

Ideally, responses to psychological scales accurately reflect people's true psychological characteristics, but participants' responses can be systematically biased in several ways. Response biases and test biases can diminish reliability and validity, potentially compromising the interpretation of research based on psychological scales.

This chapter discusses two threats to psychometric quality. First, it addresses response biases, which can compromise the meaningfulness of apparent differences among individual respondents. In addition, it describes methods of handling these biases, either by preventing or minimizing their occurrence, minimizing their effects, or detecting their occurrence. Second, the chapter addresses test bias, which can compromise the meaningfulness of apparent differences between groups of respondents. It defines the problem, and it describes methods for detecting its occurrence.

Response Bias

People's responses to a scale might be systematically biased, making their scores poor reflections of their true psychological traits or states. Whether the biases are conscious or unconscious, malicious or cooperative, self-enhancing or self-effacing, they raise concerns in psychological measurement. Motivated by these concerns, psychologists have made important strides towards understanding, detecting, and handling several response biases.

Types of response biases

A variety of response biases raise concern among developers and users of psychological scales. Some emerge from scales' content or format, some from the assessment context, some from participants' motivations to present invalid responses, and some from unconscious processes.

Acquiescence   Acquiescence or "yea-saying" occurs when respondents agree with statements (or answer "yes" to questions) without regard for the meaning of those statements or questions. Similarly, "nay-saying" occurs when respondents disagree with statements (or answer "no" to questions) without regard for content. Although some researchers doubt the existence or impact of response biases, evidence indicates that acquiescence bias exists and can affect psychological measurement (e.g., Knowles & Nathan, 1997). It is most likely when items are complex or ambiguous, testing situations are distracting, or respondents otherwise have difficulty understanding the material (Paulhus, 1991).

If acquiescence bias occurs, then researchers might fail to differentiate acquiescent responders from valid responders who have a high level of the construct being assessed. This possibility arises when all of a scale's items are scored in the same direction (i.e, when all or most are positively keyed or are negatively keyed; see Chapter 3). In such cases, a set of agreements or "yeses" from a participant could reflect either a valid set of responses or an acquiescence bias. Consequently, a high scale score might not truly reflect a high level of the underlying construct.

An important confound can arise when acquiescent participants respond to multiple scales. In such cases, participants responding acquiescently to one scale are likely to respond acquiescently to another, increasing their scores on both. If multiple scales are indeed affected, then their scores will be more positively correlated than are their intended constructs. Thus, a correlation between two scales might be "more positive" than the true correlation between constructs, leading to inaccurate psychological conclusions.

Extremity   Extremity bias refers to differences in participants' willingness to use extreme response options. Many scales are based upon statements or questions eliciting responses in terms of one's degree of intensity, endorsement, or occurrence. For example, a typical Likert-type scale might include items such as "In most ways my life is close to my ideal" with response options such as "strongly agree," "agree," and "slightly agree" (Diener et al., 1985). Obviously, "strongly agree" reflects more extreme or intense agreement than the other options. For such items, one participant might be more willing to respond in a more "extreme" way (e.g., answering "strongly agree") than another participant, even if they have the same level of the underlying construct.

This bias creates problems when: a) people with identical construct levels differ in their willingness to use extreme response options; or b) people with different construct levels do not differ in their willingness to use extreme response options. Such problems can distort true psychological similarities or differences. In research contexts, this obscures the apparent associations between constructs. And this, of course, can produce inaccurate research conclusions.

Concerns about the extremity bias are well-founded. Research reveals that differences in participants' use of extreme response options are stable across measures and across time, although some studies have failed to replicate this effect.

Social desirability   The social desirability response bias is the tendency to respond in a way that seems socially appealing, regardless of one's true characteristics. Participants sometimes respond in ways that enhance desirable qualities or that diminish negative qualities. When responses are affected by desirability biases, they fail to reflect accurately the intended constructs, which, of course, compromises psychometric quality. Although some researchers argue that social desirability bias is not as problematic as is often assumed, many remain concerned about its effects.

There are several possible sources of socially-desirable responding. First, scale content can trigger it—some psychological attributes have clear implications for social appeal, and measures of those attributes might be particularly affected by social desirability. Second, the assessment context might affect social desirability. Socially-desirable responding might be most likely when respondents can be identified or when important consequences are at stake (e.g., hiring). A third potential source is respondents' personality. Decades of research indicate that some people are more likely to respond in socially-desirable ways than are others.

Unfortunately, social desirability bias can compromise research results and conclusions. Of most concern may be that differences in participants' tendency to respond in socially-desirable ways can create spurious or artificially-strong correlations between scales. This can occur if: a) participants differ in their motivation to appear socially desirable; and b) two or more attributes are linked to social desirability. In such circumstances, participants with social-desirability motivation would have generally higher scores on the desirability-loaded scales than the participants with no social-desirability motivation. This inflates the correlation between the two measures, in comparison to the true correlation between the attributes assessed by those scales.

There may be several forms of social desirability bias (Paulhus, 2002). Impression management occurs when respondents intentionally attempt to seem socially desirable, and self-deception occurs (unintentionally) when respondents have overly-positive self-perceptions and respond accordingly. Interestingly, impression management biases might be state-like, being triggered by relevant situational demands (e.g. while completing a personnel selection inventory in a hiring context). In contrast, self-deception biases seem to be stable, trait-like differences among people, affecting responses across many different measurement contexts.

Malingering   Many psychologists worry about exaggeration of socially-appealing qualities, but others worry about the opposite problem—in some measurement contexts, respondents might exaggerate socially-unappealing or problematic qualities. When benefits might arise from being deemed cognitively impaired, emotionally distressed, or psychologically disturbed, some people might engage in malingering or "faking bad." This is likely more of a concern in applied testing than in social/personality research, so interested readers are directed to other sources for details (e.g., Rogers, 2008).

Careless or random responding Whether due to carelessness or to a lack of motivation, participants might respond randomly or semi-randomly. Obviously, this can generate meaningless scale scores.

Guessing Guessing can affect tests with items scored as correct or incorrect. This is particularly problematic when scores have important consequences for participants (e.g., college admissions). Because this problem is unlikely to affect much social/personality research, I will not discuss it in depth.

Methods for coping with response biases

Concerns about response biases have motivated development of strategies for coping with problems such as acquiescence and social desirability. As Figure 6.1 (adapted from Furr & Bacharach, 2008) illustrates, there are at least three general goals in coping with response biases, along with three general strategies.

		Goals		
		Prevent or minimize the existence of bias	**Minimize the effects of bias**	**Detect bias and intervene**
Strategies	**Manage the measurement context**	Anonymity Minimize frustration Warnings		
	Manage scale content or scoring	Simple items Neutral items Forced choice Minimal choice	Balanced scales Corrections for guessing	Embedded validity scales
	Specialized scales			Desirability tests Extremity tests Acquiescence tests

Figure 6.1 Methods for coping with response bias

Minimizing the existence of bias by managing the assessment context Ideally, researchers could prevent response biases from occurring, or at least reduce the likelihood of occurrence. Focussing on the assessment context, some strategies manage the way in which scales are presented to respondents or manage the demands placed upon the respondent. For example, assurances of anonymity might minimize socially-desirable responding, although they might increase random responding. Alternatively, creating environments that minimize respondent fatigue, stress, distraction, or frustration might maintain attention and motivation, thereby minimizing socially-desirable responding, random responding, and other biases. Thus, researchers might strive for brief measurement periods and for measurement environments that are comfortable, quiet, and free of distractions. Finally, researchers might warn respondents that the validity of their responses can be evaluated, and this might minimize socially-desirable responding or malingering. Even if researchers cannot actually detect invalid responses, the warning itself can minimize some biases.

Minimizing the existence of bias by managing scale content   To minimize the existence of response biases, researchers can manage scale content by using specific kinds of items or response formats. For example, as mentioned in Chapter 3, researchers should generate items that are straightforward and simple. Such items might avoid respondent frustration, fatigue, and distraction, thereby minimizing carelessness, poor motivation, and, ultimately, biased responding. Another strategy is to generate items that are neutral in terms of social desirability. Although there are limits to this, an item such as "I don't like to help people" might be replaced by an item such as "It is sometimes too much trouble to help people." Of course, the item's meaning changes somewhat, but the second item might be more palatable to more respondents.

Researchers can also use response formats to minimize response bias. For example, "forced choice" items present two characteristics (e.g., "Creative" and "Generous") and require respondents to choose the one that is more characteristic of them. If the characteristics are equally desirable or undesirable, then participants cannot simply make the more desirable choice. In addition, researchers can use dichotomous items (e.g., true/false, yes/no) to eliminate extreme responding, though it also affects the potential for valid differences in extremity to emerge.

Minimizing the effects of bias by managing scale content or scoring   Even if researchers cannot prevent or minimize the occurrence of response biases, they might manage scale content or scoring to minimize the *effect* of biases. For example, as mentioned earlier (Chapters 2 and 3), balanced scales minimize the possibility that acquiescence bias will confound acquiescence with truly high levels of the construct being assessed. In addition, researchers can use specialized scoring procedures, such as adjustments for guessing (as is done in scoring the SAT).

Managing test content to detect bias and intervene   As a final way of handling response biases, researchers might manage scale content in order to detect biased responses, subsequently discarding those responses or instituting statistical controls. For example, several well-known measures of psychopathology and personality include validity scales—sets of items embedded in larger inventories. Validity scales are intended to detect whether a respondent exhibits specific response biases, and an enormous amount of work has focussed on creating and evaluating validity scales for measures such as the MMPI, the MCMI, the NEO-PI, and the CPI. Although some research fails to support the utility of such scales, much evidence supports the "validity of validity scales" (e.g., Baer & Miller, 2002).

Upon identifying individuals who might have responded in a biased way, researchers have several options. First, they can retain the scores and acknowledge the fact that response biases might affect their results in various ways. Second, they can discard the individuals' scores from any analysis. Third, they can retain the data but statistically account for the fact that some respondents might have provided invalid responses. Procedures such as partial correlation or multiple regression can be used to "statistically control" for potentially biased responses (i.e., by entering validity scale scores as a control variable). The second and third options are preferable to the first.

Using specialized scales to detect bias and intervene Similar to validity scales embedded within longer measures, stand-alone scales have been designed to measure response biases. For example, the Marlowe–Crowne Social Desirability Scale (Crowne & Marlowe, 1960) and the Brief Inventory of Desirable Responding (BIDR; Paulhus, 1991) are widely-used measures of social desirability. In addition, scales have been developed to measure acquiescence and extremity biases (Couch & Keniston, 1960; Greenleaf, 1992).

As with the embedded validity scales, specialized measures of response biases can be used in a variety of ways—they allow test-users to identify and eliminate potentially invalid responses, and they allow researchers to statistically control the effects of response biases. In addition, they have been used to study response biases as phenomena in their own right. Furthermore, researchers who construct and evaluate scales can use the specialized "bias scales" to gauge the degree to which response biases might affect the scales. Such information can reveal problems and guide improvements (e.g., rewriting items to avoid social desirability issues).

Test Bias

Whereas response biases systematically obscure the psychological differences among respondents, test bias systematically obscures the differences (or lack thereof) among *groups* of respondents. If research conclusions or real-life decisions are based upon scales having differential meaning or quality in different groups, then those differences have extremely important theoretical, personal, and (potentially) societal implications.

There are at least two types of test bias. Construct bias occurs when a scale has different meanings for two groups, in terms of the construct it assesses—that is, a scale might reflect the same construct to differing degrees in two groups, or it might even reflect meaningfully-different constructs. Predictive bias, in contrast, occurs when a scale's use has different implications for different groups. It concerns the association between scores on two different measures—one of which (the predictor scale) is believed to provide values that predict scores on the other (the outcome or criterion measure). Predictive bias occurs when the association between predictor scores and outcome scores differs across groups. The two types of bias are independent—a given scale could have one but not the other. For example, the SAT might accurately reflect true "academic aptitude" differences within two groups of people (and thus have no construct bias), but academic aptitude might not be associated with freshman GPA equally for two groups of people (and thus predictive bias would exist).

The importance of test bias

Test bias has important implications for research and applied measurement. In research contexts, it can compromise the examination of groups' mean differences and the examination of group differences in correlations.

For examinations of mean differences in groups' scale scores, researchers would like to assume that a scale measures a given construct equally well in two groups. That is, researchers would like to assume that all groups' scale means are *equally good* reflections of their true means. If this assumption is valid, then a comparison of groups' scale means can be interpreted as a valid comparison of the groups' true means. However, if a scale suffers from test bias, then the groups' scale means are not equally-good reflections of their true means, and comparisons of scale means cannot be interpreted as valid comparisons of true means.

For examinations of group differences in correlations, researchers correlate a scale with one or more other variables within each group and compare the groups' correlations. For example, researchers might study cultural differences in the association between income and well-being. Thus, they might correlate the Satisfaction with Life Scale (SWLS) with income in a Western sample and in an Eastern sample, intending to compare the two correlations. If, for example, the observed correlation is larger in the Western sample, then they might conclude that income has a greater association with well-being in the Western culture than in the Eastern. However, this comparison hinges on the assumption that observed scores on SWLS reflect true well-being equally well in both samples. Unfortunately, if the SWLS suffers from culture-based test bias, then this assumption is invalid, and a comparison of the correlations cannot be interpreted as a comparison of the true psychological associations between income and well-being.

In applied contexts, test bias can compromise the legitimacy of decisions based upon test scores, with some groups undeservedly benefitting over others. Ideally, test scores allow decision-makers to differentiate among people based on true psychological differences, but test bias can produce apparent differences that do not reflect real psychological differences. In such cases, reliance upon test scores can produce psychologically-invalid group disparities in decision-making. Such possibilities are of crucial concern when psychological tests are used to inform decisions such as hiring, promotion, and admissions.

Given the importance of test bias, some effort has been dedicated to minimizing the existence or effects of test bias; however, most effort has been dedicated to procedures for detecting bias. Importantly, the existence of group differences in scale scores *does not* necessarily imply that the scale is biased—an observed difference in scale scores can, in fact, reflect true psychological group differences. In such cases, the scale is not biased. Psychometricians have developed procedures for detecting both construct bias and predictive bias.

Detecting construct bias

Researchers evaluate construct bias by examining responses to scale items. An item is biased if: a) people from different groups respond in different ways to the item; and b) these differing responses are not due to group differences in the construct assessed by the scale. For example, imagine an item from a scale measuring Neuroticism, and imagine that females, on average, endorse the item to a greater degree than do males. If females and males do not truly differ on Neuroticism, then this item is gender-biased. Further, if one or more items are biased, then the scale might suffer from gender-based test bias.

There are several procedures through which researchers can estimate the existence and degree of construct bias. Generally speaking, they involve examination of a scale's internal structure separately for two groups. If groups have dissimilar internal structures in their scale responses, then researchers conclude that the scale likely suffers from construct bias. There are at least four such procedures (see Furr & Bacharach, 2008)—item discrimination indices, rank order of item difficulties, differential item functioning (see Chapter 10), and factor analysis.

For example, by factor-analyzing items separately for two or more groups, researchers can evaluate the presence and nature of construct bias. Construct bias could be revealed in several ways. First, groups might differ in the number of factors underlying responses to scale items. For example, factor analysis might reveal a unidimensional structure within one group but a two-dimensional structure within another. In such case, the scale's items clearly have different psychological implications in the groups, and they should be scored and interpreted differently in the two groups. Second and more subtly, groups might have differing associations between items and factors. For example, factor analysis might reveal a two-factor structure in each group, but the pattern of factor loadings in one group might differ meaningfully from the pattern in the other. In such cases, the scale's items might reflect importantly-different psychological attributes, and they should not be scored or interpreted similarly.

A closely-related issue is differing reliability. If a scale is substantially more reliable in one group than in another (e.g., .80 in one group and .60 in another), then the scale reflects its construct more precisely in one group than in another, raising two potentially-serious problems for examination of differential correlations. First, differing reliability could produce group differences in observed correlations when, in fact, there are no group differences in true-score correlations. This could happen if the groups have similar true-score correlations, but relatively poor reliability in one group attenuates that group's observed correlations to a greater degree than the other group. Second, differing reliability could produce similar observed correlations in two groups, when in fact there *are* group differences in true-score correlations. This could happen if the groups have dissimilar true score correlations, but relatively poor reliability in the "larger true correlation" group attenuates its observed correlation to a level that is similar to that of the other group. Thus, researchers should carefully examine reliability when comparing correlations between groups. For example, they might use the correction for attenuation (Equation 4.3) to estimate the true correlation in both groups and then compare those values (at least descriptively).

Detecting predictive bias

As mentioned, predictive bias concerns the degree to which a scale is equally predictive of an outcome for two groups. For example, if the SAT predicts college GPA more strongly for females than for males, then it might suffer from gender-based predictive bias. Predictive bias is usually examined via regression analysis.

Examination usually begins by establishing statistically what would happen if no bias exists. If a scale is unbiased, then one regression equation should apply to all groups of respondents. That is, researchers begin by assuming that "one size fits all" and evaluating a common regression equation across all groups. For example, a researcher might use regression to predict college GPA from SAT scores for a sample including females and males. The key results of this analysis are called the common intercept and the common slope. If the SAT has no gender bias, then the common regression equation should be equally applicable to males and females separately.

To determine whether the common regression equation is indeed equally applicable, researchers conduct regression analysis for each group. If group-level results differ from the common regression equation, then SAT scores may be biased. For example, group-level regression analyses might reveal that females and males have slopes matching the common slope but that the females' intercept is larger than the males' intercept (with the common intercept between the two). Such "intercept bias" implies that females at any given level of SAT will tend to earn higher GPAs than will males who have the same level of SAT scores. Similarly, group-level regression analyses might reveal that the females' intercept and slope are larger than the males' values. Such results could mean that both the degree and direction of bias varies across levels of the scale scores. For example, results might reveal that at some specific SAT-levels, females at that level are likely to earn higher GPAs than are males at that level, but that at other SAT-levels, females at that level are likely to earn *lower* GPAs than are males at that level. Thus, regression can reveal simple or complex patterns of potential predictive bias.

Other statistical procedures

Although it is beyond the scope of the current discussion, additional statistical procedures can be used to detect test bias. For example, Item Response Theory, Confirmatory Factor Analysis, and structural equation modeling can yield data related to test bias, or "measurement invariance." In addition, hierarchical regression procedures allow researchers to test specific hypotheses about the sources of predictive bias.

Summary

This chapter has addressed issues that threaten the psychometric quality of scale scores and the clarity of their psychological meaning. Response biases such as acquiescence bias and social desirability bias systematically obscure psychological differences among individuals, or they artificially create apparent differences where none truly exist. Similarly, test biases obscure psychological differences among groups of people, or they artificially create apparent group differences where none truly exist. Researchers have developed procedures for handling or detecting both types of problems. Researchers and readers should always be aware of these potential threats and consider their implications for statistical results and psychological conclusions.

Note

1 This chapter addresses several factors that contribute to biased responding. Some factors might be temporary, reflecting the assessment situation (e.g., important consequences hinge on the measurement) or the scale itself (e.g., test format or ambiguity of items). Such factors are sometimes called "response sets." Other factors reflect stable characteristics of individuals (e.g., general concern about appearing socially desirable), and they are sometimes called "response styles." Thus, response biases arise from response sets (i.e., something about the testing situation produces biases) and response styles (i.e., something about a person being tested produces biases), but psychologists are inconsistent in their use of these terms.

7

Difference Scores

This chapter addresses an important but somewhat misunderstood issue in psychological measurement—difference scores. Many interesting psychological phenomena can be seen as differences between two "component" phenomena. For example, a participant's actual–ideal discrepancy might be viewed as the difference between his or her actual standing on a variable and his or her preferred standing on that variable. Similarly, researchers studying psychological change might measure participants' level of self-esteem at one point in time, measure their self-esteem again at a later time, and interpret the differences as indications of "amount of change in self-esteem" for each participant. Or finally, one's "attractiveness range" might be viewed as the difference between the thinnest body type (say, as reflected in Body Mass Index) that one finds attractive and the heaviest body type that one finds attractive. For such phenomena, researchers might be tempted to use difference scores—measuring each component variable (e.g., BMI of the thinnest body type that a person finds attractive and BMI of the largest body type he or she finds attractive) and then subtracting one value from another to produce a difference score (also called change scores, gain scores, and discrepancy scores).

Difference scores are intuitively appealing. They seem to fit well with phenomena such as actual–ideal discrepancy, psychological change, and attractiveness range, and they arise from simple subtraction:

$$D_i = X_i - Y_i \qquad \text{(Equation 7.1)}$$

An individual's difference score is the difference between his or her score on two components—variable X and variable Y. Given this intuitive appeal and simplicity, difference scores have been used in many areas of psychology, including social and personality psychology.

Although difference scores are appealing, they entail complexities that, if not understood and managed, can compromise researchers' conclusions. The psychometric complexities of differences scores have been discussed for decades, and the complexities can work in various ways—producing effects that are misleadingly complex, spuriously large, inaccurately small, or in the wrong direction completely. If the issues are ignored, then research quality suffers—perhaps producing conclusions that are misinformed or that simply miss more fundamental phenomena.

These complexities are particularly problematic when examining predictors (i.e., correlates or group differences) of difference scores. For example, a researcher might be interested in understanding the factors that make men attracted to a wider range of body sizes, hypothesizing that men's Extraversion is related to their attractiveness ranges (i.e., that extraverted men will be attracted to a wider range of body types than will introverted men). To evaluate this hypothesis, researchers might be tempted to create an "attractiveness range" difference score for each male participant, as described earlier, and correlate these scores with the participants' extraversion scores. A significant positive correlation might lead them to conclude that, indeed, high levels of extraversion are predictive of attraction to a wide range of body sizes. However, careful analysis may reveal simpler, clearer, and more fundamental messages. For example, careful analyses might reveal that extraversion is indeed related to attraction to heavier women but not to thinner women. That is, extraverted men might be more attracted to heavier women than are introverted men, but no more attracted to thinner women than are introverted men.

This chapter presents psychometric and statistical properties of difference scores, important implications of these properties, problems arising from these implications, and recommendations regarding difference scores. The practical take-home message is twofold:

1 Researchers should consider avoiding difference scores, instead focussing on the component variables from which difference scores are computed.
2 If researchers use difference scores, then they should do so with thorough examination of the component variables and with serious attention to psychometric quality.

Properties of difference scores

There are at least two fundamental statistical/psychometric properties of difference scores—properties with implications for the meaning of difference scores and, ultimately, for conclusions based upon difference scores. The properties concern the reliability and variability of difference scores.

Reliability   Observed difference scores are treated as indicators of "true" psychological difference scores. That is, the observed difference between measured variable X and measured variable Y is taken as an indicator of the difference between a person's true score on variable X and his or her true score on variable Y. Thus, it is important to understand the factors affecting the reliability of observed difference scores—factors affecting the degree to which variability in observed difference scores reflects variability in true difference scores.

In theoretical terms, the reliability of observed difference scores (r_{DD}) is affected by true score variability in the component variables, the true correlation between component variables, and the reliability of the measures of the component variables:

$$r_{DD} = \frac{s_{T_X}^2 + s_{T_Y}^2 - 2s_{T_X}s_{T_Y}r_{T_XT_Y}}{\dfrac{s_{T_X}^2}{r_{XX}} + \dfrac{s_{T_Y}^2}{r_{YY}} - 2s_{T_X}s_{T_Y}r_{T_XT_Y}}$$ (Equation 7.2)

In this equation, $s_{T_X}^2$, $s_{T_Y}^2$, s_{T_X}, and s_{T_Y} are the true score variances and standard deviations of variables X and Y (the two components of the difference score), r_{XX} and r_{YY} are reliabilities of the measures of X and Y, and $r_{T_XT_Y}$ is the true correlation between X and Y.[1] As we will see, this equation has important implications for the meaning and utility of difference scores.

Variability   Most analyses of difference scores focus on their observed variability. In an experimental context, one might evaluate whether experimentally-induced differences in one or more IVs explain variability in participants' observed difference scores. In a non-experimental context, one might evaluate whether naturally-occurring differences in one or more predictor variables are associated with variability in participants' observed difference scores. The importance of variability in difference scores requires an understanding of the factors producing that variability. Specifically, variability in observed difference scores reflects variability in component measures and the correlation between those measures:

$$s_D^2 = s_X^2 + s_Y^2 - 2r_{XY}s_Xs_Y$$ (Equation 7.3)

where s_D^2 is the variance of observed difference scores, s_X^2, s_Y^2, s_X, and s_y are the observed variances and standard deviations of measures of variables X and Y, and r_{XY} is the correlation between those measures.

Implications of these properties

These properties reflect fundamental statistical and psychometric qualities of difference scores, and they have several implications. These implications, in turn, affect the meaningfulness and utility of difference scores.

Unreliable scales produce unreliable difference scores   There is much debate about the reliability of difference scores. Some researchers believe that difference scores are inherently unreliable, while others note that difference scores can, in fact, be reasonably reliable. Difference scores can indeed be reliable, but only when their component measures are reliable.

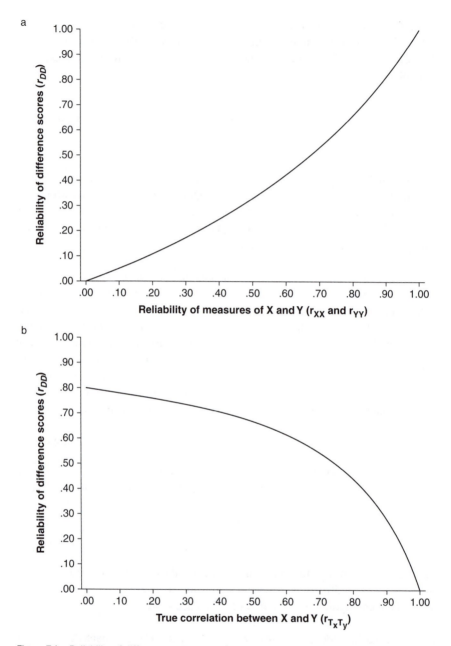

Figure 7.1 Reliability of difference scores as a function of: a) reliabilities of components, and b) true correlations between components

Based upon Equation 7.2, Figure 7.1a reflects the reliability of difference scores as a function of the reliability of component measures. Values were generated by holding constant the true correlation between X and Y (arbitrarily) at $r_{T_X T_Y} = .50$, holding equal the true variances of X and Y (i.e., $s_{T_X}^2 = s_{T_Y}^2$), and assuming that measures of X and Y are equally reliable. As the figure shows, components with low reliability produce difference scores with very poor reliability—e.g., if r_{XX} and r_{YY} are .40, then $r_{DD} = .25$. However, components with strong reliability can produce difference scores that are reasonably reliable—e.g., if r_{XX} and r_{YY} are .90, then $r_{DD} = .82$. Thus, difference scores *can* be reliable, but only if one or both components are highly reliable.

Highly-correlated components produce unreliable difference scores   Perhaps somewhat counterintuitively, the reliability of difference scores is reduced when components are positively correlated with each other. Equation 7.2 reflects the reliability of difference scores as a function of the true correlation between the components (i.e., $r_{T_X T_Y}$), and Figure 7.1b illustrates this across a range of true correlations. This figure (which assumes that X and Y have equal true variances and that their measures have reliabilities of .80) shows that larger inter-component correlations produce smaller reliabilities of difference scores. For example, it shows that components that are truly correlated with each other at only $r_{T_X T_Y} = .10$ can produce difference scores with good reliability of $r_{DD} = .78$; however, components that are correlated more robustly with each other, say at $r_{T_X T_Y} = .70$, produce difference scores with substantially lower reliability, $r_{DD} = .54$. That is, difference scores have lower reliability when components are highly positively correlated (even though both component measures might be highly reliable). This fact leads some researchers to question the reliability—perhaps even the utility in general—of difference scores.

Difference scores can simply reflect one of the components   Although difference scores arise from two component variables, variability in difference scores can simply reflect variability in one component. That is, under some circumstances, difference scores reflect—or largely reflect—one component. This implication is apparent in the correlation (r_{XD}) between the difference scores and one component (in this case, variable X):

$$r_{XD} = \frac{s_X - r_{XY} s_Y}{\sqrt{s_X^2 + s_Y^2 - 2r_{XY} s_X s_Y}} \qquad \text{(Equation 7.4)}$$

where s_X^2, s_Y^2, s_X, and s_y and r_{XY} are as defined earlier. This equation shows that the correlation between a difference score and a component is affected by the difference between the variabilities of the two components. That is, for any given level of association between components (i.e., holding r_{XY} constant), difference scores are more strongly linked to the component with greater variability. In sum, if components have different variabilities, then the one with greater variability will have greater impact on the difference scores (see Equation 7.3) and thus will be more strongly correlated with difference scores (Equation 7.4).

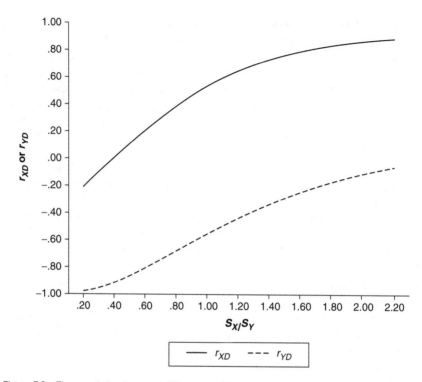

Figure 7.2 The correlation between difference scores and their component variables, as a function of the relative sizes of the components' variabilities

This effect can be seen in Figure 7.2, which presents correlations between difference scores and each component variable (i.e., r_{XD} and r_{YD}). Correlations are presented as a function of the ratio of variability in component X to variability in component Y (i.e., s_X/s_Y) and (arbitrarily) setting the components correlated with each other at $r_{XY} = .40$. When component X has less variability than component Y (e.g., when $s_X/s_Y = 0.2$), difference scores are less strongly correlated with component X than with component Y (i.e., $r_{XD} = -.21$ and $r_{YD} = -.98$). In contrast, when component X has *greater* variability than component Y (e.g., when $s_X/s_Y = 2.0$), difference scores are *more* strongly correlated with component X than with component Y (i.e., $r_{XD} = .87$ and $r_{YD} = -.10$). It is only when the components have equal variability that they are equally correlated with difference scores (i.e., if $s_X/s_Y = 1$, then $|r_{XD}| = |r_{YD}|$).

Issues in application of difference scores

Thus far, this section has presented key psychometric properties of difference scores along with three implications of those properties. In addition, my experience as a reviewer, editor, and reader suggests three observations of the way that difference scores are sometimes applied in social/personality research:

1 Difference scores are derived occasionally from "single-item" component measures, with little, if any, attention to psychometric implications. This problem compounds an issue mentioned earlier in this volume—single-item measures are relatively likely to have poor psychometric quality. Thus, difference scores based upon single-item component measures are likely to have very poor psychometric quality.
2 Despite long-held concerns regarding the reliability of difference scores and despite the importance of knowing the psychometric quality of any variables being examined, researchers often seem to ignore the reliability of difference scores.
3 Despite the strong dependence of difference scores upon their components, researchers sometimes ignore the components when examining difference scores. That is, researchers seem to move quickly to analysis of difference scores, bypassing the fact that difference scores simply reflect their components to varying degrees.

Potential problems arising from difference scores

Taken together, the properties, implications, and applied issues produce significant concerns with the use of difference scores. Three problems are particularly important, potentially compromising research based upon difference scores.

Poor reliability may obscure real effects   Although reliability might be less pervasively problematic than sometimes supposed, there are legitimate concerns about the reliability of difference scores. As mentioned earlier, the reliability of difference scores suffers when components are correlated positively with each other and when those components are measured with poor reliability. In many, perhaps most, applications of difference scores, components are likely to be robustly correlated with each other. When combined with the possibility that difference scores are sometimes derived from components having poor (or unknown) reliability, this creates significant potential problems with the reliability of difference scores.

If difference scores have poor reliability, then subsequent analyses may miss meaningful and real effects. As discussed earlier (Chapter 4), poor reliability reduces observed effect sizes, which reduces the power of inferential analyses, which increases the likelihood of Type II errors. These effects are as true for difference scores as they are for any variable.

Lack of discriminant validity, producing obscured results   Perhaps the most subtle problem is that difference scores can lack discriminant validity, potentially obscuring psychological conclusions based upon their analysis. Because difference scores can be influenced heavily by a component having relatively large variance, they can simply reflect one component. This psychometric situation could produce conclusions that poorly reflect psychological reality—that are misleading, overly complex, obscure, or that simply miss deeper psychological messages.[2]

For example, a recent study of perceived physical attractiveness presented personality correlates of "attractiveness range" difference scores (Swami et al., in press). In this research, male participants viewed images of nine increasingly-large female figures, which were interpreted as a 1–9 interval scale of size. Each participant identified the smallest and largest figures he found attractive, and the difference (in terms of the size-scale values) was interpreted as a participant's "attractiveness range" (AR). AR difference scores were then correlated with scores from personality scales, producing a significant negative correlation between AR and Extraversion. This seemingly suggests a meaningful connection between males' Extraversion and the range of body sizes they find attractive—extraverted males seem to be attracted to a "narrower range of body sizes" than do introverted males.

However, deeper analysis clarified and fully explained the apparent "attractive-ness range" findings. Specifically, the "largest attractive" ratings had much greater variability than did the "smallest attractive" ratings. That is, males varied much more dramatically in the largest-sized figures they found attractive than in the smallest-sized figures they found attractive. As discussed earlier, if one component of a difference score has greater variability than the other, then the difference score largely reflects the one with greater variability. Consequently, AR difference scores largely reflected the "largest attractive" ratings, as verified by an extremely high correlation ($r = .86$) between the difference scores and the "largest attractive" ratings (Swami et al., in press). Fortunately, the researchers examined the components (i.e., smallest attractive and largest attractive ratings) alongside the difference scores (i.e., AR scores), revealing the confounding of AR scores with one of its components. This allowed more informative and psychologically-meaningful interpretations than would have been possible with only the analysis of difference scores. Reliance upon only the AR difference scores would have produced conclusions that were limited reflections of the psychological reality otherwise readily apparent in the analysis of the two components.

This potential obscuring effect can be seen in the correlation (r_{PD}) between a predictor or independent variable (e.g., Extraversion) and a difference score (e.g., AR):

$$r_{PD} = \frac{r_{PX}s_X - r_{PY}s_Y}{\sqrt{s_X^2 + s_Y^2 - 2r_{XY}s_X s_Y}} \qquad \text{(Equation 7.5)}$$

In this equation, r_{PX} and r_{PY} are correlations between the predictor and component variables, and s_X^2, s_Y^2, s_X, s_y, and r_{XY} are as defined earlier. The numerator reveals that the association between a predictor/IV and a difference score is largely a blend of correlations between the predictor/IV and the components. More deeply, all else being equal, the association reflects a link between the predictor/IV and whichever component has greater variability. Thus, in the AR study, the association between Extraversion and AR largely reflected a link between Extraversion and the "largest attractive" ratings.

Results and conclusions can change dramatically, based upon meaningless differences in variability Finally, difference scores can produce results that can change in size, significance, and even direction, depending on potentially-meaningless differences in the components' variances or on arbitrary decisions about scaling or scoring tests. More technically, analyses based upon difference scores are not invariant across linear transformations of the components, and such transformations—though psychologically meaningless—can thus produce dramatic changes in one's psychological conclusions.

For example, researchers might hypothesize that people who experience a large number of negative life events show greater personality change than do people who experience fewer life events. To examine this hypothesis, they might measure Neuroticism at Time 1, Neuroticism at Time 2, and "Number of negative life events" during the two time points.

To examine these data, researchers might be tempted to compute a "change score" for each participant by subtracting Time 1 Neuroticism scores from Time 2 Neuroticism scores. Such difference scores seem to reflect both the direction and amount of change in Neuroticism for each person (e.g., a large positive value seemingly indicates that an individual's Neuroticism increased dramatically). Researchers might then be tempted to conduct analyses in which they examine the correlation between "Number of negative events" and "change in Neuroticism." Analysis might reveal a robust positive correlation (say, $r = .47$, $p < .05$), leading the researchers to conclude that experiencing a relatively large number of negative events is associated with increases in Neuroticism.

However, imagine that researchers then discover a simple, relatively meaningless scoring issue. Specifically, they discover that, unlike the "Time 1 Neuroticism" responses, the "Time 2 Neuroticism" scale responses were summed instead of averaged. In terms of the fundamental meaning of scale scores, this "issue" is meaningless. That is, summed scores are just as psychologically meaningful as are averaged scores. Obviously, participants who have relatively high summed scores are exactly those who would have relatively high average scores—in fact, the correlation between summed scores and averaged scores is $r = 1.0$. Thus, there is no psychologically meaningful difference between participant's "Time 2" summed scores and their "Time 2" averaged scores—there is no inherent reason to average rather than sum responses. Nevertheless, there is a discrepancy between the two sets of "component" scores—although each component's scores are psychologically meaningful in their own right, they are scaled on arbitrarily different metrics (one set is summed and the other is averaged). This creates problems for the analysis differences between the two sets of scores.

Discovering this discrepancy, researchers re-score the Time 2 Neuroticism scale by averaging responses. They then re-create the "change" scores, correlate the new

Table 7.1   Example data

Participant	T2Neur (summed)	T1Neur	Number of events	Original difference score	T2Neur (averaged)	Adjusted difference score
1	20	1.6	1	18.4	1.33	−.267
2	45	2.6	4	42.4	3	.4
3	45	5.3	6	39.7	3	−2.3
4	44	3	3	41	2.93	−.067
5	24	2.8	2	21.2	1.6	−1.2
6	39	3.8	4	35.2	2.6	−1.2
7	65	5.3	5	59.7	4.33	−.967
8	32	2	3	30	2.13	.133
9	70	4.6	3	65.4	4.67	.067
10	90	6.5	4	83.5	6	−.5

change scores with "Number of negative life events," and obtain a very robust *negative* correlation ($r = -.51$, $p < 05$). They thus conclude that experiencing a relatively large number of negative events is, in fact, associated with *de*creases in Neuroticism. See Table 7.1 for the hypothetical data that produces these results.

So which result is correct—do negative events increase or decrease Neuroticism? Both conclusions are based upon analyses of three variables that, on their own, are entirely legitimate and meaningful. Indeed, the discrepancy in conclusions emerges from a psychologically meaningless scoring discrepancy.

In this case, it might seem obvious that the "correct" result is the one based upon the similarly-scored results. However, this example reflects a deeper problem—the results of analysis based upon difference scores are affected by differences in the variances of the component variables (see Equation 7.5). Such differences in variance might well be meaningless in general or in terms of the supposed meaning of difference scores. Analysis of difference scores will reflect most heavily whichever component variable has greater variability—even if the difference in variability is psychologically meaningless. Thus, differences in variability can have serious and meaningful effects on psychological conclusions based upon analyses of difference scores. Fortunately, there are informative alternatives to difference scores.

Recommendations and alternatives

Given the potential problems associated with difference scores, researchers might consider several alternatives and suggestions. There are at least two alternatives to difference scores, and there are several recommendations that should be strongly considered if difference scores are used.

Partial one component from the other   Perhaps the best alternative to difference scores is an approach in which one of the components is partialled (Cohen & Cohen, 1983). It can be accomplished via regression (or ANCOVA) by treating one component as an outcome and treating the other component as a predictor in a model along with another predictor of interest (i.e., a variable hypothesized to be related to the difference).

For example, consider again the hypothesis that people who experience many negative events show greater personality change than do people who experience fewer events. After measuring the three relevant variables (i.e., Neuroticism at Time 1, Neuroticism at Time 2, and "Number of significant life events"), researchers could first examine the bivariate associations between the predictor of interest (i.e., "Number of events") and both Neuroticism scores. This reveals the most fundamental information regarding personality and number of events, and it provides important context for interpreting any subsequent analyses (as will be discussed).

After examining bivariate associations, researchers could enter the main predictor of interest and "Time 1 Neuroticism" as predictors in a regression model with "Time 2 Neuroticism" as the outcome variable:

Mode 1: Time 2 Neuroticism $= a + b_1$ (Time 1 Neuroticism) $+ b_2$ (Number Events).

The size and significance of the slope for "Number of events" reveals the degree to which people who experience a large number of life events have increased in their level of Neuroticism. More specifically, a large, positive, significant slope indicates that, for two people who began the study with the same level of Neuroticism, the one who experienced a larger number of life events is likely to have a higher level of Neuroticism at the end of the study.

There are at least three important things to realize about this analytic approach. First, unlike difference scores, the key results from this approach are completely unaffected by differences in variances of the components. Specifically, the direction of the predictor's slope (i.e., b_2 in the model above), all relevant standardized coefficients (i.e., the standardized regression coefficient, the partial correlation coefficient, and the semi-partial correlation coefficient), and the significance test of the slope/coefficients are all invariant over linear transformations of either, or both components. Thus, the fact that the components might differ in their variabilities has no implications for this analytic approach. Consequently, potentially meaningless differences in variability have no effect on researchers' conclusions based upon this analytic approach.

Second, some of the most fundamental results of this approach remain the same even if a slightly different (but equivalently meaningful) model is examined. Specifically, researchers might choose to examine this model:

Model 2: Number Events $= a + b_1$ (Time 1 Neuroticism) $+ b_2$ (Time 2 Neuroticism).

Here the components are predictors, the other variable of interest is the outcome, and the key information comes from coefficients related to "Time 2 Neuroticism." Importantly, the partial correlation coefficient and the significance test associated with "Time 2 Neuroticism" in this model are identical to those associated with the "Number Events" predictor in Model 1. Thus, both models reflect the association between "Number of events" and "Time 2 Neuroticism" while controlling for "Time 1 Neuroticism," and their key results converge both in terms of an effect size (i.e., partial correlation) and inferential statistic.

A third important facet of this approach is that it can be examined via multilevel modeling (MLM). As a relatively new statistical procedure, MLM (see Nezlek, 2011, part of this series) is useful for analyses of intra-individual differences or change. An extensive discussion is beyond the scope of this volume, but it is worth noting that MLM can handle these procedures and important extensions.

Examine each component as a dependent variable A second alternative to difference scores is to again avoid difference scores altogether, focussing instead on separate analysis of the components. For example, researchers might conduct analyses twice—once with each component as a dependent variable. Anything potentially revealed in an analysis of difference scores might be revealed more clearly, simply, and directly by analysis of the two components. Note that this approach can, in fact, be a precursor to the first alternative discussed above.

Consider a regression context, though the same principles apply in ANOVA contexts. Rather than examining a single "difference score model" in which difference scores are predicted by a predictor variable (i.e., $D_i = a + b_{PD}(P_i)$), researchers could examine two "component models," $X_i = a + b_{PX}(P_i)$ and $Y_i = a + b_{PY}(P_i)$, predicting each component (X and Y) from the predictor variable (P). The slopes from the component models reflect the association between each component and the predictor, and the difference between these slopes is identical to the slope obtained from the difference score model (i.e., $b_{PD} = b_{PX} - b_{PY}$). Similarly, as shown earlier (Equation 7.5), the correlation between a predictor variable and a difference score (r_{PD}) largely reflects the difference between the two component–predictor correlations (r_{PX} and r_{PY}, weighted by the components' standard deviations). Similar ANOVA approaches could be used, or perhaps even more usefully, an ANOVA approach can be translated into a regression analysis. Important generalizations of this approach are presented by Edwards (1995).

Such examination of components rather than difference scores potentially reveals important information and avoids problems associated with difference scores. For example, if the predictor is related strongly to only one component, then a separate-component analysis would reveal this fact. Similarly, if components differ in their variability, then separate-components analysis avoids the discriminant validity problem arising with difference scores (i.e., the difference score primarily reflecting the component having greater variability). Note however, that the unstandardized slopes (i.e., between b_{PX} and b_{PY}) are affected by differences in the components' variances—thus, the apparent differences in these coefficients are not invariant over linear transformations of the components.

Examine difference scores along with their components   After considering alternatives, some researchers might remain interested in difference scores. If difference scores are used, then they should be used only when accompanied by careful examination of component scores.

At a minimum, researchers using difference scores should present fundamental psychometric information and descriptive statistics of the components and of difference scores. Specifically, they should present: a) reliability estimates of the components and of difference scores; b) the means and variabilities of the components and of difference scores; and c) the correlation between the two components and the correlation between each component and the difference scores. Researchers can estimate the reliability of difference scores via:

$$estimated\ r_{DD} = \frac{s_X^2 \left(estimated\ r_{XX}\right) + s_Y^2 \left(estimated\ r_{YY}\right) - 2s_X s_Y r_{XY}}{s_X^2 + s_Y^2 - 2s_X s_Y r_{XY}} \qquad \text{(Equation 7.6)}$$

where s_X^2, s_Y^2, s_X, s_y, and r_{XY} are as defined earlier. Thus, researchers can use the components' basic descriptive and psychometric information to estimate the reliability of difference scores.

Such information allows researchers and readers to gauge potential problems with reliability and discriminant validity. If reliabilities appear low, then researchers should consider the resulting limitations upon their ability to detect meaningful results. Further, if one component has substantially-greater variability than the other, then researchers should recognize the resulting lack of discriminant validity between the "larger variability" component and the difference score. A lack of discriminant validity would be apparent also in a large correlation between that component and the difference score. If such validity-related concerns exist, then readers and researchers should interpret analysis of difference scores very cautiously. In fact, such findings might motivate researchers to avoid difference scores altogether, returning to a separate-component approach.

Going further, researchers using difference scores should also conduct all analyses with both components (i.e., running three sets of analysis). For example, the "attractiveness range" research (Swami et al., in press) presented one set of analyses with the difference score as the dependent variable, another analysis with the "thinnest-size deemed attractive" component as the DV, and another with the "largest-size deemed attractive" component as the DV. Results revealed no effects for the "thinnest" component, significantly robust effects for the "largest" component, and significantly robust effects for the difference score. The latter finding is fully predictable from the fact that previously-reported correlational analysis revealed an extremely large association between the "largest" component and the difference scores. That is, the IV's effects on the "attractiveness range" difference score simply reflect the IV's effects on the "largest" component. The authors noted this important fact when discussing their results.

Summary

The intuitive appeal of difference scores masks a psychometrically-thorny set of problems. This chapter introduced psychometric properties of difference scores, noted important implications and potential problems arising from these properties, and presented analytic recommendations. In sum, there are important psychometric and statistical concerns about difference scores, and alternatives should be considered. Analysis of difference scores—if conducted at all—should be conducted only alongside analysis of the components producing the difference score, and only with careful attention to core psychometric issues.

Notes

1 Equation 7.2 differs from some equations articulating the reliability of difference scores, such as this commonly-presented equation:

$$r_{DD} = \frac{1/2\left(r_{XX} + r_{YY}\right) - r_{XY}}{1 - r_{XY}}$$

This equation is accurate when the component measures have equal variabilities—a situation that, though sometimes true, bypasses crucial psychometric facts. In contrast, Equation 7.2 follows the basic tenets of classical test theory, with no additional assumptions or constraints, and it reveals implications regarding the links between variability and reliability.

2 Interestingly, difference scores are the basis of some familiar statistical procedures, such as the test of an interaction in a split-plot analysis. Note that such analysis requires attention to the homogeneity of variances of the within-subjects factor, corresponding to concern about the similarity of variances of the two components of a difference score. Furthermore, researchers would rarely limit analysis to a significant interaction, more likely proceeding to decompose the interaction into simple main effects. Such informative, important, and quite standard follow-up analysis parallels the examination of the two components of a difference score.

8

Confirmatory Factor Analysis

As discussed earlier, researchers can use factor analysis to evaluate the internal structure, or dimensionality, of a psychological scale. The previous discussion highlighted Exploratory Factor Analysis (EFA) as useful when researchers have few, if any, hypotheses about a scale's internal structure. In contrast, Confirmatory Factor Analysis (CFA) is useful when researchers have clear (or competing) hypotheses about a scale—the number of factors or dimensions underlying its items, the links between items and factors, and the association between factors.

Recall that a scale's dimensionality or internal structure has implications for reliability, validity, and scale use. A scale's internal structure is relevant to its reliability, reflecting the scale's internal consistency by revealing which items are consistent with which other items. Similarly, a scale's internal structure is relevant to validity, because the appropriate interpretation of its scores hinges on the match between its internal structure and the internal structure of its intended construct(s). Following from these implications, a scale's internal structure has implications for its construction and scoring. That is, scale construction is informed by awareness of internal structure—either in terms of tailoring a scale to fit a structure of interest (e.g., to reflect five dimensions of personality or one global dimension of self-esteem) or in terms of understanding the psychological phenomenon being assessed by the scale's items. Correspondingly, scale use is informed by internal structure, in terms of scoring the scale in a way that generates reliably meaningful indicators of one or more psychological constructs. Given the psychometric importance of internal structure, CFA is a potentially important psychometric tool.

Partly due to increasing availability and user-friendliness of advanced software, CFA is indeed an increasingly-popular tool for scale construction and psychometrics. In many examples of such work, researchers produce multi-study articles tracing a scale's development and evaluation (e.g., Leach et al., 2008), including analyses of the scale's internal structure, often through both EFA and CFA. After clarifying the scale's structure, they then examine the reliability and validity of each dimension through a series of studies.

This chapter reviews basic issues in the logic of CFA, the analytic process, and the key results. Although CFA is most directly relevant for evaluating internal structure, it also provides information about internal consistency, and it can be used to evaluate convergent and discriminant evidence. The latter issues will be covered toward the end of this chapter. This chapter is intended to be relatively non-technical, with additional depth available in other sources (e.g., Thompson, 2004; Brown, 2006; Hoyle, 2011, part of this series), including some tailored to popular software packages (Hatcher, 1994; Diamantopoulos & Siguaw, 2000; Byrne, 2001, 2006).

The Process of CFA for Analysis of a Scale's Internal Structure

Overview of CFA and example

With CFA, researchers evaluate "measurement hypotheses" regarding a scale's internal structure. That is, CFA allows researchers to evaluate the degree to which their measurement hypotheses are consistent with actual data produced by respondents. By examining three key sets of results—parameter estimates, fit indices, and, potentially, modification indices—researchers formally test measurement hypotheses, and they can modify hypotheses to be more consistent with the actual structure of participants' responses to the scale. Furthermore, researchers often examine multiple measurement hypotheses to identify the one that best matches participants' actual responses. Thus, CFA facilitates theory-testing, theory-comparison, and theory-development in a measurement context.

Figure 8.1 outlines a CFA process. The discussion below describes the steps in this process, highlighting the logic of each and the psychometric information that is produced and typically reported. The figure differentiates steps in which researchers have active roles (the unshaded boxes) from those performed by the statistical software (in shaded boxes). The figure also shows that CFA is often an iterative process in which a scale's hypothesized measurement model is articulated, evaluated, revised, and re-evaluated. Ultimately, researchers report information about the model-testing process, including any revisions to the model(s), with primary attention to the model that best matches the scale's actual internal structure.

To illustrate these issues, the discussion below highlights an example provided by Leach et al. (2008). This research addressed the conceptualization and measurement of in-group identification—the degree to which individuals identify with in-groups. The primary goal was to evaluate the hypothesis that in-group identification includes five components (e.g., Individual Self-Stereotyping, Solidarity), with a secondary goal of developing a scale measuring those components. Of seven studies reported by the authors, the first two were CFA-based examinations of the hypothesized multi-factor measurement model.

Preliminary steps

Before conducting CFA, researchers conduct at least two important preliminary steps. First, of course, is initial development of a scale, as outlined in Chapter 3.

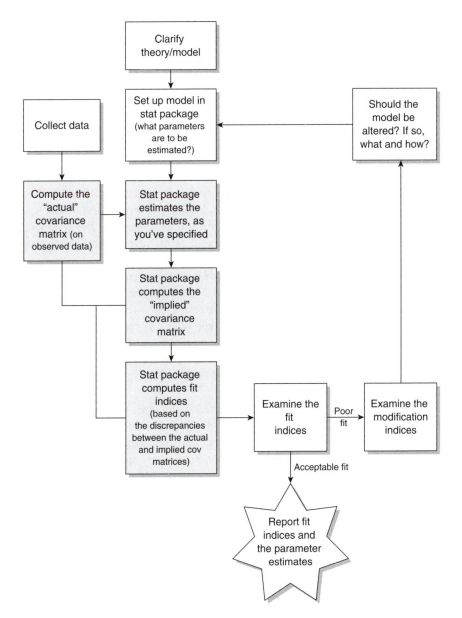

Figure 8.1 Flowchart of confirmatory factor analysis and structural equation modeling

Indeed, Leach et al. (2008) describe a conceptually-oriented item generation and evaluation process producing 14 items intended to reflect five components integral to in-group identification. A second preliminary step is collection of responses to the scale. Leach and his colleagues recruited two samples of approximately

400–500 respondents to complete their 14-item questionnaire. The appropriate sample size for CFA is a complex issue. Recommendations for absolute sample sizes vary from a minimum of 50 participants (with simple models under ideal conditions) to 400 or more, while other recommendations are framed as "participants-to-variables" ratios with suggestions ranging from 5:1 to 20:1 or more. Before CFA analysis, responses to negatively-keyed items should be reverse-scored.

Step 1: Specification of Measurement Model

After initial item writing and data collection, researchers articulate the measurement model within CFA-capable software. Software packages such as AMOS/SPSS, SAS, and LISREL have made the process fairly easy, allowing researchers simply to draw diagrams reflecting their measurement models. The following discussion highlights psychometrically-relevant facets of model-articulation or "specification."

Researchers specify at least three facets of a measurement model, as summarized in Table 8.1 and illustrated in Figure 8.2 (adapted from Leach et al., 2008). First, they specify the number of factors or latent variables (represented by ovals) hypothesized to underlie the scale's items (represented by rectangles). For example, Figure 8.2a reflects a unidimensional measurement model in which 14 items are hypothesized to load on a single factor. In contrast, Figure 8.2b reflects a multidimensional model in which items load on five factors, which in turn reflect two more fundamental factors.

Second, researchers specify the items linked to (i.e., that load on) each factor, with at least one item linked to each factor (though this is not necessarily true for hierarchical measurement models, as we shall see), and with each item typically linked to only one latent variable. Typically, researchers specify that particular items are associated with particular latent variables, though the precise association will be estimated by the software. That is, they hypothesize that participants' responses to particular items are affected by the participants' levels of particular

Table 8.1 Facets of the measurement model to be specified by researchers

Facets
Required specifications:
1 Number of factors
2 The associations between items and factors
3 The potential associations between factors (if more than one factor is hypothesized)
Examples of some additional specification options:
4 Exact values of one or more parameters (e.g., specific factor loading values)
5 Equality of parameters (e.g., two factor loadings constrained to be equal)

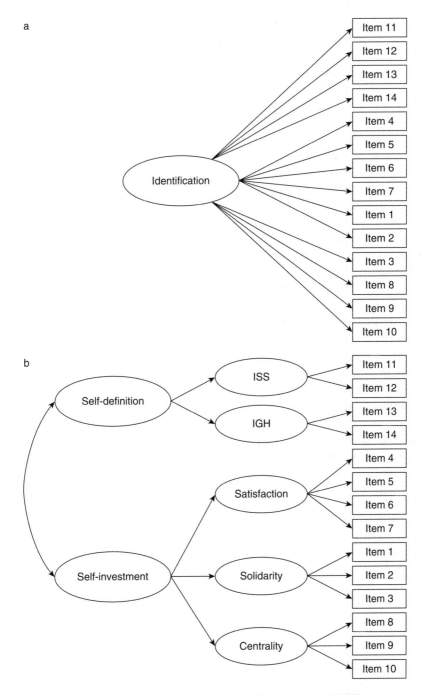

Figure 8.2   Example: two measurement models examined by Leach et al. (2008)

latent variables, and they allow the software to estimate the strength of these effects. In addition, when working with multidimensional models, researchers specify that particular items are not associated with one or more latent variables. That is, they specify that items have a zero-loading on one or more latent variables. For example, the multidimensional model in Figure 8.2b hypothesizes that items 11 and 12 load only on an Individual Self-Stereotyping factor and that items 4, 5, 6, and 7 load only on a Satisfaction factor. Essentially, a pathway (i.e., arrow) between an item and a factor indicates a hypothesized non-zero association between the two; correspondingly, the lack of a pathway indicates a hypothesized zero association.

Third, if a hypothesized model includes multiple factors, then researchers specify possible associations between factors. There are two ways of representing hypotheses that factors are associated with each other. First, factors may load on a "higher-order" factor. Figure 8.2b presents a hierarchical measurement model in which two "lower-order" factors—ISS and IGH—load on a higher-order factor called Self-definition. That is, an individual's levels of ISS and IGH are hypothesized to be affected by his or her level of Self-definition. If two or more factors are hypothesized to be affected by a higher-order factor, then, by extension, those lower-order factors are assumed to be associated with each other. The second way in which researchers can represent a hypothesized association among factors is by having factors simply be correlated with each other. For example, the two-way arrow between Self-definition and Self-investment in Figure 8.2b indicates a hypothesis that those factors are correlated with each other. In contrast, the lack of an arrow or pathway between factors indicates a hypothesis that they are uncorrelated. Figure 8.2b implies that all factors are hypothesized to be correlated with each other to some degree—for example, ISS and Satisfaction are hypothesized to be correlated because ISS potentially loads on Self-definition, which is potentially correlated with Self-investment, which affects Satisfaction.

Typically, at least three types of measurement-related parameters are requested during model-specification. These are among the key results to be interpreted, used (potentially) for model revision, and ultimately reported by researchers. First, specification identifies the hypothesized factor loadings to be estimated. When researchers hypothesize that an item loads on a factor, they typically do not hypothesize a specific value. Rather, they request that the loading's value be estimated by the software. These loadings—again, usually one per item—reflect the degree to which each item is linked to a psychological construct presumably being measured by the scale. A second type of parameter often requested, at least for multidimensional scales, is the correlation between factors or the loading of a lower-order factor on a higher-order factor. Again, when researchers hypothesize that one factor loads on another or when they hypothesize that two factors are correlated, they typically do not hypothesize specific values; rather, they obtain estimates from the software. Third, researchers implicitly request estimates of error variance for each item. That is, they often request that the software estimates the amount of each item's variance that is unrelated to the substantive factor hypothesized to affect the item. Note that these values are not always reported, as researchers focus more commonly on the first two types of parameter estimates. In sum, these three types of parameters are often "freely-estimated," in that researchers essentially state that "these parameters are probably not zero" and allow software to estimate the parameters' precise values.

Step 2: Analysis

After specifying the hypothesized model, researchers submit their specifications and their scale's data for analysis, and the software goes to work. A quick overview of this statistical process may provide greater understanding of CFA's key results. Analysis can be seen, roughly, as a four-phase process.

In the first phase, the software uses the collected data to compute the items' actual variances and the actual covariances among the items. This information will be used to estimate item parameters and to gauge the model's accuracy.

In the second phase of the analysis, the software uses items' actual variances and covariances to estimate parameters as specified by the researcher. For example, it uses the actual association between two items to estimate the factor loadings that they might have on a common factor. Such information is used to estimate all factor loadings, inter-factor correlations, error variances, and so on. In addition to estimating parameters, software computes inferential statistics for each parameter. For the typical inferential test of a parameter, the null hypothesis is that the parameter is zero in the population. For example, the software tests all hypothesized factor loadings, evaluating whether each item loads significantly on its factor.

In the third phase, the software uses the estimated parameters to create "implied" item variances and covariances. Based upon statistical rules linking parameters to item variances and covariances, it produces item variances and covariances as implied by the specified model and its estimated parameters. If the model is good (i.e., if it is a good approximation of the true factor model underlying the scale's items), then the implied variances and covariances will match closely the actual variances and covariances computed in the first phase of analysis. If the model is poor, then the implied values will differ greatly from the actual values.

In the fourth phase, the software generates information reflecting the overall adequacy of the hypothesized model. More specifically, it compares the implied variances/covariances to the actual variances/covariances, computing indices of "model fit" and modification. Small discrepancies between implied and actual values produce indices of "good fit," suggesting that the hypothesized measurement model adequately accounts for the associations among the scale's items. In contrast, large discrepancies produce indices of "poor fit," suggesting that the hypothesized measurement model does not adequately account for the scale's data. Many "fit indices" are computed by popular software, and several will be discussed later. Going further, "modification indices" reveal specific ways in which the hypothesized measurement model might be modified. More specifically, they indicate potential modifications that would make the hypothesized factor structure more consistent with the factor structure that truly may be underlying the scale's items. For example, a modification index derived from analysis of Figure 8.2b might suggest that item 11 loads the IGH factor. The original model does not hypothesize that item 11 loads on IGH, so researchers might consider modifying their hypothesis to accommodate this suggestion.

Step 3: Interpreting and Reporting Output

After researchers gather responses to a scale, specify a measurement model hypothesized to underlie those responses, and conduct analyses, they interpret output and, depending on the results, report their findings. CFA produces output relevant to many facets of the analysis and of the model itself. This section describes some of the most relevant and commonly-reported results. As shown in Figure 8.1, the particulars of this step and the next hinge on the pattern of the results. Depending on some results, researchers might or might not examine additional results, and they might conclude their analyses or extend them. In best-case scenarios, hypothesized measurement models closely match actual responses to scales, and researchers need to examine only two sets of output.

Fit indices Typically, researchers first examine fit indices reflecting the overall adequacy of the hypothesized measurement model. As described earlier, "good fit" indicates that the hypothesized measurement model is consistent with observed data, providing support for that model. In contrast, "poor fit" indicates that the hypothesized measurement model is inconsistent with observed data, and it is interpreted as evidence against the adequacy of the model.

Despite the availability of many indices, researchers seem to concentrate on only a few, though there are differing preferences. Perhaps the most commonly-examined index is chi-square, which indicates the degree of mis-fit of the model. Small, non-significant chi-square values indicate little mis-fit, providing support for a hypothesized measurement model. In contrast, large significant chi-square values indicate large mis-fit, providing evidence against the hypothesized model. This "significant is bad" interpretation of chi-square differs from the typical perspective on inferential statistics, in which researchers generally hope for significant effects. Although chi-square is usually examined and reported in CFA, researchers and readers should recall that sample size affects chi-square. As with any inferential procedure, large samples produce large chi-square values, which produce statistical significance. This creates a paradox for CFA—large samples are required in order to obtain robust, reliable parameter estimates, but large samples also increase the likelihood of significant chi-square values indicating inadequacy of a hypothesized model. For this reason (among others), researchers examine additional indices of model fit—most of which are not formal inferential statistics. For example, researchers examine indices such as the Goodness of Fit Index (GFI), the Incremental Fit Index (IFI), the Normed Fit Index (NFI), the Comparative Fit Index (CFI), the Non-normed Fit Index (NNFI; also known as the Tucker–Lewis Index or TLI), the Root Mean Square of Approximation (RMSEA), the Root Mean Square Residual (RMR), the Standardized Root Mean Square Residual (SRMR), and the Akaike Information Criterion (AIC), to name but a few. The various fit indices have differing scales and norms for indicating model adequacy—for example, large values of the GFI (up to 1.0) indicate good fit, but small values of the RMR (down to 0) indicate good fit. Many sources provide guidance for interpreting the various fit indices (e.g., Kline, 1998; Hu & Bentler, 1999).

For example, Leach and colleagues (2008) begin reporting CFA results by presenting fit indices for the multidimensional model in Figure 8.2b (their primary model of interest). For participants' responses to in-group identification as "University students," Leach et al. reported seven fit indices—chi-square, CFI, NFI, GFI, SRMR, RMSEA, and AIC. Results are summarized in the "8.2b" column of Table 8.2. Upon finding CFI, NFI, and GFI values above .930 and SRMR and RMSEA values below .08, the researchers concluded that Model 8.2b fit their scale's data. In addition, they reported the significant chi-square but reminded readers of the link between large sample sizes and statistical significance, and they noted that "[m]easurement models rarely produce nonreliable chi-squares in samples of this size" (p. 150). Such dismissal of significant chi-square values seems standard in many CFA analyses.

To more fully evaluate their main model of interest, Leach et al. (2008) presented fit indices for several alternative measurement models, including the unidimensional model in Figure 8.2a. Analysis of this model indicated poorer fit—see the "8.2a" column in Table 8.2. Specifically, poor fit is indicated by CFI, NFI, and GFI values well below the .930 benchmark cited by Leach and colleagues, by SRMR and RMSEA values well above a .08 benchmark, and by an extremely large chi-square value. Considering the fit indices for their main hypothesized measurement model (Model 8.2b) and for several alternative measurement models (such as Model 8.2a), the researchers concluded that the measurement model in Figure 8.2b was the most strongly-supported model of their scale.

As shown in Figure 8.1, fit indices lead researchers in one of two directions. If they indicate that the model is adequate, then researchers will likely examine parameter estimates to evaluate specific psychometric qualities of the scale. If instead they indicate that the model is inadequate, then researchers will likely examine modification indices to consider potential revisions to the model.

Table 8.2   Fit indices for two measurement models examined by Leach et al. (2008)

Fit index	Measurement model		Cited benchmark
	8.2b	8.2a	
χ^2	212.09*[a]	1807.60*[b]	NA
CFI	.967	.600	> .93
NFI	.952	.591	> .93
GFI	.938	.629	> .93
SRMR	.051	.119	< .08
RMSEA	.066	.220	< .08
AIC	70.09	1653.60	NA

Notes: *$p < .05$, [a]$df = 71$, [b]$df = 77$. Benchmarks are those cited by Leach et al. (2008)

Parameter estimates   Upon concluding that a measurement model has an acceptable overall fit, researchers typically examine and report parameter estimates such as the items' factor loadings, the inter-factor associations, and error variances. A value is obtained for each parameter that the researcher asks the software to estimate, with no estimates provided for parameters that the researcher has hypothesized to be zero. Parameter estimates are important information regarding the scale's factorial structure and psychometric properties.

As described earlier, factor loadings reflect the degree to which each item is linked to a factor. That is, an item's factor loading reflects the degree to which differences among participants' responses to the item arise from differences among their levels of the underlying psychological construct being assessed by that item. If an item is hypothesized to load on a particular factor, then researchers hope to find a significantly-large positive factor loading. If such results are found, then researchers will likely retain that item. If, however, an item is hypothesized to load on a factor but its factor loading is small and/or non-significant, then researchers will likely conclude that the item is unrelated to the factor, removing it from the scale. In such cases, they might re-specify the model to fit the revised scale (i.e., eliminating the item from the model) and re-run the analysis to evaluate the revised scale. This scenario might seem paradoxical—a generally well-fitting model combined with a weak factor loading; however, it is important to recognize that fit indices (e.g., GFI) reflect the overall adequacy or fit of the entire measurement model. Thus, a model can indeed have generally good support, despite having some weak specific aspects.

Continuing the example from Leach et al. (2008), Figure 8.3 presents some key parameter estimates for their main hypothesized measurement model (i.e., Figure 8.2b). Because this model received support from the fit indices reported in Table 8.2, the researchers interpreted and reported its parameter estimates. As shown by the standardized loadings in Figure 8.3, items loaded well on the five lower-level factors—for example, item 11 loaded at .93 on the ISS factor, and

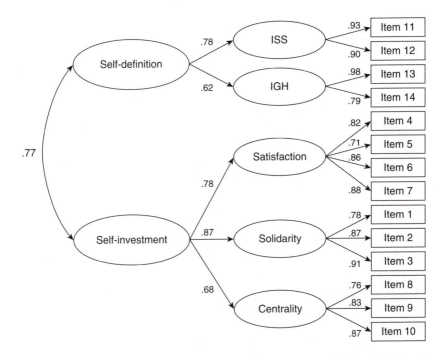

Figure 8.3   Measurement model 8.2b with parameter estimates reported by Leach et al. (2008)

item 13 loaded at .98 on the IGH factor (note that standardized loadings can be interpreted on a roughly correlational metric). The researchers noted the magnitude (all > .60) and significance of these factor loadings, concluding that they "confirmed that each of the five components was well defined by its items" (p. 150).

When a measurement model includes multiple factors, researchers also interpret and report parameters reflecting associations among factors. As discussed earlier, inter-factor associations can be modeled either as the effects of higher-order factors on lower-order factors, or as the correlations between factors. If higher order factors are hypothesized to affect lower-order factors, then researchers expect significantly large "inter-factor loadings" (i.e., the loading of a lower-order factor on a higher-order factor). Similarly, if factors are hypothesized to be non-causally associated with each other, then researchers expect significantly-large inter-factor correlations.

Again, Leach et al. (2008) provide relevant examples. As shown in Figure 8.3, each lower-order factor loads strongly on its hypothesized higher-order factor. For example, the lower-order ISS factor loads .78 on the higher-order Self-definition factor, and the Satisfaction factor loads .78 on the Self-investment factor. Considering the size (all > .50) and statistical significance (not reflected in Figure 8.3) of these results, the researchers concluded that "[e]ach of the five components loaded onto the expected second-order factor" (p. 150). Similarly, Figure 8.3 reveals that the hypothesized correlation between the higher-order factors was sizable and significant, leading Leach et al. to conclude that "The second-order factors of self-definition and self-investment tended to be moderately associated ..." (p. 150).

Researchers usually highlight the parameters described above—items' factor loadings and inter-factor associations. Sometimes, they also present parameters reflecting items' error variances or the item's variance-explained values. Because these values are implied by the factor loadings, researchers rarely burden readers with this additional information. Indeed, Leach et al. (2008) did not present these values.

In sum, as shown in Figure 8.1, the progression of CFA interpretation and subsequent steps hinge on several issues—most notably the overall adequacy of an initial hypothesized measurement model. If fit indices support a model, then researchers often proceed to examination of parameter estimates. If those parameter estimates are reasonable and supportive of the model (e.g., there are no weak, non-significant factor loadings), then CFA is usually considered finished. However, if fit indices provide poor support for a model, then researchers will likely revise their hypothesis, hopefully improving their understanding of the scale's true dimensionality. This raises the next potential step in CFA—model modification and re-analysis.

Step 4: Model Modification and Re-analysis (if necessary)

As Figure 8.1 illustrates, researchers sometimes, perhaps often, must consider modifying a hypothesized measurement model. When obtaining poor fit indices, researchers will likely examine modification indices to identify potentially-useful revisions to a measurement model.

Typically, each modification index refers to a parameter that was initially set to zero in a measurement model. For example, the model reflected in Figure 8.2b implies that item 11 loads on the ISS factor but not on the IGH factor. Thus, researchers initially set or "fixed" the loading of item 11 on the IGH factor to zero, creating a model in which item 11 has no direct association with IGH. When examining modification indices, researchers would find a value referring to this parameter—the "fixed-to-zero" factor loading of item 11 on IGH. Indeed, they would find modification values for every parameter that was set to zero.

The size of a modification index reflects the potential benefit of revising the relevant parameter. For parameters having large modification index values, researchers might consider revising the hypothesized measurement model in a way that changes that parameter. For example, CFA of the model in Figure 8.2b might reveal a relatively large modification index referring to item 11's potential loading on the IGH factor. If so, then researchers might revise the model by allowing item 11 to load on both the IGH factor and the ISS factor. By adding this parameter to the model (i.e., by allowing the parameter to be estimated), researchers essentially hypothesize that responses to item 11 are affected by both ISS and IGH. This change, and others indicated by relatively large modification indices, should improve the model's fit.

As Figure 8.1 shows, after examining modification indices and changing one or more parameters, researchers re-run the analysis. Analysis of revised models produces entirely new output—new fit indices, new parameter estimates, etc. Thus, researchers evaluate the adequacy of the revised model, and they either examine parameter estimates (if the revised model fits well) or new modification indices (if the model still fits poorly).

Modification indices provide potentially-useful information about a scale's factor structure, but modification blurs distinctions between confirmatory and exploratory analysis. Therefore, researchers should be wary of extensive post-hoc modifications, particularly modifications without clear conceptual rationale. Such modifications might be unstable across different samples of respondents, as they may be based upon response patterns unique to the original respondents. If more than one or two modifications are made, then researchers should strongly consider evaluating the revised model in a cross-validation sample before drawing strong inferences.

Comparing models

When conducting CFA, researchers often evaluate competing measurement models (e.g., a one-factor model versus a two-factor model). Such comparisons are based upon differences between the fits of two models—all else being equal (e.g., in terms of theoretical basis), researchers prefer measurement models with relatively good fit.

A full discussion of model-comparison processes is beyond the scope of this chapter (see Hoyle, 2011, part of this series), but, generally speaking, researchers compare fit indices for one model to those of the alternative model(s). For example, Leach et al. (2008) compared six measurement models when examining their in-group identification scale—as mentioned earlier, Figure 8.2b illustrates their primary model of interest and Figure 8.2a illustrates one of five alternative models. To compare models, Leach and his colleagues computed and reported fit indices for each model, with particular interest in each alternative model's fit as compared to the primary model. These comparisons produced support for the primary model—both on its own and in comparison to the alternative models (e.g., its CFI, NFI, and GFI values were high, its SRMR and RMSEA values were low, and its AIC value was lower than the other models' AIC values). These findings were interpreted as evidence that the primary hypothesized model was the best representation of the actual structure of responses to the in-group identification scale.

Although a full discussion is beyond the scope of this volume, model comparison can sometimes proceed through inferential tests of differences between two models' fit. If one model is "nested" within another (i.e., if one model is obtained simply by adding/removing constraints on one or more parameters), then researchers can compute a chi-square value reflecting the difference between the two models' fits (see Hoyle, 2011 for more details). The difference between chi-square values from two nested models is itself a chi-square value, and it can be tested with degrees of freedom equal to the difference between the degrees of freedom values from two nested models. If the "difference" chi-square is statistically significant, then researchers conclude that one model fits significantly better than the other.

Summary

As a psychometric tool, CFA is usually used to evaluate the dimensionality of psychological scales. By allowing researchers to test hypotheses about measurement models, CFA is an important complement to Exploratory Factor Analysis. In addition, its ability to facilitate model testing, model comparison, and model revision makes CFA a valuable tool for psychologists constructing or revising psychological scales. However, the usefulness of CFA goes beyond evaluations of dimensionality, and the following sections describe its utility for evaluating reliability and validity.

CFA and Reliability

Although coefficient alpha is a popular method of estimating reliability (see Chapter 4), its accuracy depends upon psychometric assumptions that may not be valid in some applications of behavioral research (Miller, 1995). Indeed, its accuracy is affected by the pattern and nature of items' psychometric properties (e.g., do the items have correlated errors, do they have equal factor loadings?).

Alpha's limitations have led researchers to consider factor analysis (or principal components analysis) as a vehicle for greater insight into a scale's reliability (e.g., Armor, 1974). To date, the use of CFA to evaluate reliability is rare, but researchers have recently developed reliability-estimation procedures based upon CFA. This section describes CFA-based procedures for unidimensional scales, and interested readers can find additional details and examples in several sources (e.g., Raykov, 2004; Brown, 2006, pp. 337–351).

From a CFA perspective, reliability can be estimated through a two- or three-step process (depending upon potential model modifications). In the first step, researchers conduct CFA to examine the fit of a simple measurement model. For example, Figure 8.4a presents a unidimensional model potentially representing the 8-item Extraversion scale of the Big Five Inventory (BFI; John & Srivastava, 1999). In this model, all items are hypothesized to load on one factor, without additional correlations among items. Note that this figure includes an error term affecting each item, representing the effect of random measurement error on responses to each item. Although such error terms are implicit in all CFA models, they are not always included in the models' visual presentations (e.g., see Figures 8.2 and 8.3). Based upon responses obtained from a relatively small sample of respondents (n = 115), CFA analysis suggests that the unidimensional model does not fit the Extraversion scale well—$X^2_{(20)} = 99.961$, p < .05; GFI = .782; RMSEA = .187 (analyses were conducted via SAS's "proc calis").

In the next step, researchers modify and re-analyze the measurement model if necessary. If the initial hypothesized model fits poorly, then researchers examine modification indices for useful revisions, with an eye toward associations among items' error terms. For example, examination of modification indices for the poorly-fitting model in Figure 8.4a revealed three modifications that are meaningful both conceptually and statistically (in terms of a relatively strong improvement in the model's fit). These indices suggest modifying the model by estimating the associations between error terms of the negatively-keyed items in the scale (items 2, 5, and 7). These three items are more highly correlated with each other than is implied by a simple unidimensional model that includes all eight items of the Extraversion scale. Based upon the size of the modification indices and upon the conceptually-meaningful fact that the items have a commonality (i.e., they are the scale's negatively-keyed items), the model was modified to include three relevant parameters—the pair-wise associations among the items' error terms. Re-analysis reveals that the modified model fits the scale's data quite well ($X^2_{(17)} = 26.549$, p > .05; GFI = .947; RMSEA = .070). Figure 8.4b presents the modified model and relevant unstandardized parameter estimates, including each item's factor loading, the error variance of each item, and the covariance between error terms of the three negatively-keyed items.

In the final step, unstandardized parameter estimates are used to estimate reliability, via (Brown, 2006):

$$estimated\ reliability = \frac{\left(\sum \lambda_i\right)^2}{\left(\sum \lambda_i\right)^2 + \sum \theta_{ii} + 2\sum \theta_{ij}} \qquad \text{(Equation 8.1)}$$

In this equation, λ_i reflects an item's factor loading, θ_{ii} reflects an item's error variance, and θ_{ij} reflects the covariance between the error terms of two items (note that this term is zero for models without correlated error terms). From a reliability context, $(\sum \lambda_i)^2$ reflects the variance of true scores (i.e., signal), and $\sum \theta_{ii} + 2\sum \theta_{ij}$ reflects random error variance (i.e., noise). Thus, Equation 8.1 represents the theoretical definition of reliability as the ratio of true-score variance to total observed score variance (with observed variance as the sum of true-score

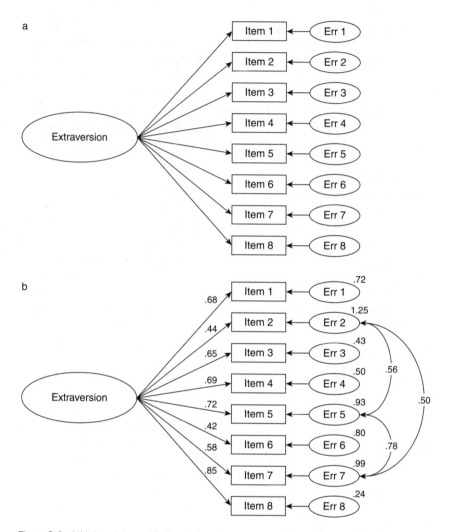

Figure 8.4   Initial model, modified model, and parameter estimates for the BFI extraversion scale

variance and error variance, see Chapter 4). For Figure 8.4, true-score variance is estimated as 25.30:

$$(\Sigma \lambda_i)^2 = (.68 + .44 + .65 + .69 + .72 + .42 + .58 + .85)^2 = 25.30.$$

Similarly, error variance is estimated as 9.14:

$$\Sigma \theta_{ii} + 2\Sigma \theta_{ij} = (.72 + 1.25 + .43 + .50 + .93 + .80 + .99 + .24) + 2(.56 + .50 + .78) = 9.14.$$

Thus, the reliability of the BFI's Extraversion scale is estimated as .73:

$$BFI\ Extraversion\ estimated\ reliability = \frac{25.30}{25.30 + 9.14} = .73$$

For these BFI data, the CFA-based reliability estimate (.73) is noticeably discrepant from the reliability estimate obtained via coefficient alpha, $\alpha = .84$. According to arguments cited earlier (e.g., Miller, 1995), this discrepancy reflects alpha's tendency to mis-estimate reliability.

CFA can produce even more useful information regarding a scale's reliability. For example, CFA can be used to estimate reliability for multidimensional scales, to estimate group differences in reliability, and to obtain confidence intervals around estimates of reliability (e.g., Raykov, 2004). Indeed, CFA is an important alternative to alpha for estimating reliability of psychological scales.

CFA and Validity

CFA can be useful for evaluating scale validity in several ways. First, by providing critical information regarding dimensionality, CFA offers insight into the "internal structure" aspect of validity. That is, CFA is a powerful tool for evaluating the validity of hypotheses about a scale's structure (i.e., does the actual structure fit the structure implied by the theoretical basis of the intended construct?).

Second, when a scale is examined alongside measures of other constructs or criteria, researchers can evaluate its association with those variables. Whether this associative evidence is viewed as convergent/discriminant validity, concurrent validity, criterion validity, predictive validity, or external validity, it affords insight into the psychological meaning of the construct(s) being assessed by the scale. There are at least two ways of using CFA to evaluate a scale's associations with other constructs or criteria.

One way to use CFA for evaluating convergent and discriminant validity is by applying it to multi-trait multi-method matrices (MTMM, Chapter 5). Recall that an MTMM study includes multiple traits/constructs (e.g., Extraversion, Neuroticism, Openness to Experience), each of which is assessed via multiple methods (e.g., self-report, peer-report, parent-report). By examining associations among all measures, researchers can evaluate convergent validity, discriminant validity, method effects, and other important validity information. Researchers have explored the application of CFA to MTMM data, developing several CFA-based methods of evaluating an MTMM matrix (see Chapter 6 of Brown, 2006).

A second way to use CFA for insight into convergent and discriminant validity is through focussed examination of a particular scale and one or more criterion variables. For example, researchers might evaluate the construct validity of the BFI Extraversion scale by collecting participants' self-reports on the scale along with participants' "extraverted" behavior in three videotaped social situations. With such data, researchers have several analytic options and potential questions— does the BFI Extraversion scale have a unidimensional structure as hypothesized, to what degree do participants' behavior scores from the three situations reflect a single extraverted behavior factor, and to what degree is the BFI Extraversion factor associated with a potential extraverted behavior factor? The latter two questions reflect the fact that construct validity hinges not only on the scale in question, but also upon the accuracy of the theoretically-based hypothesis about the link between a scale and a criterion measure and upon the psychometric quality of the criterion measures (see Chapter 5 of this volume; John & Benet-Martinez, 2000). CFA offers the capability of accounting for all of these issues, for example by examining a model illustrated in Figure 8.5. In such a model, a measurement model for the BFI Extraversion scale is hypothesized, a measurement model for the criterion is hypothesized (i.e., all three situational extraversion scores load on a single behavioral extraversion latent variable), and the correlation between the scale and the criterion is estimated. Through well-articulated analyses of such models, researchers can evaluate validity evidence in terms of the estimated correlation between a scale and criterion, while accounting for measurement error in both the scale and the criterion. This is an important advantage of CFA over many alternative analytic strategies (e.g., the zero-order correlation between scale scores and criterion scores). Such models and similar ones (e.g., Figure 2 in McArdle, 1996) extend CFA to Structural Equation Modeling (SEM), but the basic principles described in this chapter apply to SEM as well as CFA. Again, readers interested in additional details of SEM are directed to a variety of useful sources (e.g., Hoyle, these volumes).

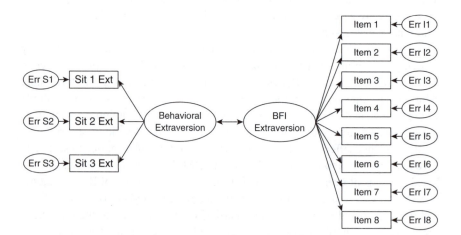

Figure 8.5 A model to evaluate associative validity

Summary

With increasing availability and user-friendliness of software capable of conducting latent variable analyses, CFA can be a useful and accessible tool for psychologists constructing or evaluating psychological scales. CFA offers researchers power and flexibility in evaluating the dimensionality of their scales, the reliability of their scales, and, ultimately, the validity of their scales. Indeed, CFA has advantages over other statistical techniques (e.g., EFA and regression) and indices (e.g., coefficient alpha). Although it requires greater thought and attention than do some other psychometric tools, CFA's advantages should be considered carefully by all researchers whose work hinges on clear understanding of their scales, questionnaires, tests, and other measures (i.e., all researchers who measure psychological variables). Several sources provide important recommendations regarding the conduct and reporting of CFA analyses (e.g., Jackson et al., 2009).

9

Generalizability Theory

This chapter introduces Generalizability Theory (G-Theory; Cronbach et al., 1972) as a psychometric tool that can be very useful for psychologists. G-Theory can be seen as an expansion of Classical Test Theory (CTT; see Chapter 4), providing a powerful method of addressing many issues, including the quality and meaning of psychological measurements. This chapter describes fundamental concepts in G-Theory, which essentially integrates CTT with Analysis of Variance, and it illustrates G-Theory analysis, emphasizing the rationale, process, calculations, and interpretations. Interested readers can find greater detail and depth in other sources (e.g., Shavelson & Webb, 1991; Brennan, 2001).

Basic Concepts

Facets of measurement designs

For some psychological scales, variability in participants' scores is potentially affected by several facets of the measurement process, which in turn might affect measurement quality. G-Theory is applicable to measurement strategies in which single *or* multiple facets might influence measurement quality, enabling researchers to disentangle effects of different facets on the measurement's overall quality. In contrast, CTT cannot differentiate among facets, limiting researchers' ability to understand the properties of multiple-facet measurement designs.

For example, imagine a psychologist studying pro-social behavior. Her participants engage in 10-minute video-recorded interactions with a confederate who relates a story of personal misfortune, and she wishes to measure the degree to which participants exhibit pro-social behavior in response. She might opt to use either a single-facet measurement design or a multiple-facet design.

Single-facet designs   Using a single-facet strategy, the researcher can use "direct behavioral observation" (Furr, 2009; Furr et al., 2010) by recruiting three assistants to watch all interactions and rate the degree to which each participant "expresses concern" (on a 7-point Likert-type scale). The researcher could average the three ratings for each participant, forming an aggregated score reflecting pro-social behavior. This is a "single-facet" strategy because it includes only one property that varies systematically—raters. That is, it included no other characteristics that systematically varied with more than one level or form—it included multiple raters, but only one item, only one situation (i.e., conversation with an ill-fortuned confederate), only one point in time, etc.

Given this single-facet design, the researcher can examine the degree to which variability in that facet (i.e., raters) systematically affects measurement quality. Specifically, because the design includes three raters, she can examine differences among the raters' data. As we have seen, such information can be used to evaluate and perhaps improve the measurement process. Indeed, both G-Theory and CTT are useful psychometric tools for such evaluation. However, because this is a single-facet design, the researcher can examine only differences related to that facet—she can evaluate measurement only in terms of raters. Because the design included only one item, she cannot use her data to explore and evaluate differences among items that could be used to evaluate pro-social behavior. Similarly, because the design included only one situation, she cannot evaluate measurement-related differences among situations in which pro-social behavior might be expressed. Such issues could be examined if the measurement design includes additional facets.

Multiple-facet designs For an alternative measurement strategy, the researcher might use a two-facet design in which three raters observe all interactions, rating each participant's behavior in terms of several items ostensibly reflecting pro-social behavior—"expresses concern," "exhibits compassion," and "offers support." She might adopt this multiple-facet design due to concerns about using only one item to reflect pro-social behavior. That is, she might worry that one item would capture only a narrow part of pro-social behavior, or she might be concerned that any given item has potentially ambiguous meaning.

In this multiple-facet design, two properties vary systematically—raters and items. This allows the researcher to evaluate the degree to which differences in both facets affect behavioral ratings. For an even more complex design, the researcher might video-record participants in two social situations—a conversation with an ill-fortuned confederate and an aggressive confederate. For such a study, she might ask three raters to provide ratings (using all three items) after watching each of the two situations.

Although CTT is useful for single-facet measurement designs, it cannot differentiate facets efficiently in multiple-facet designs. According to CTT, variance in a measure's observed scores is differentiated into only two components: true score variance and error variance. From this perspective, error variance is undifferentiated. That is, CTT cannot differentiate the effects of multiple facets, such as raters and items—any such effects are pooled into a single "measurement error" component. For example, the hypothetical researcher's two-facet design produces nine ratings of each participant's behavior—three raters each rating three items. Within a CTT approach, these ratings might be treated as nine "tests" of pro-social behavior—there is no efficient way to differentiate the effects of rater-differences from the effects of item-differences.[1]

In contrast, G-Theory is applicable to single-facet *and* multiple-facet measurement designs. This broad applicability arises because G-Theory conceptualizes measurement error as potentially differentiated. As a psychometric framework, G-Theory can be used to investigate more than one systematic difference among the properties of a measurement design, revealing the effects that the different aspects have on the overall quality of the measure (including potential interactive effects).

Thus, G-Theory a powerful tool for theoretical and practical examinations of measurement. For example, the researcher might have theoretical interest in the degree to which people have differing perceptions of pro-social behavior. Therefore, she might conduct a study in which several perceivers watch people interact and then rate the interactants' pro-social behavior. For this study, she wishes to disentangle differences among perceivers from the differences among behavioral items. The researcher might also have practical interest in disentangling raters and items as facets of the measurement process. For instance, she might wish to develop an efficient but reliable measurement procedure for a large-scale study. In terms of both time and money, relying on multiple raters might be more costly than relying on multiple items—each additional rater (e.g., going from 2 to 3 raters) might be more expensive and time-consuming than simply requiring each rater to rate additional items (e.g., going from 3 to 5 items). To evaluate various measurement designs for the large-scale study, the researcher can conduct a small pilot study consisting of several raters and several items. G-Theory allows her to examine these data and evaluate the psychometric quality of various combinations of numbers of raters and numbers of items (e.g., 3 raters each rating 4 items, or 2 raters each rating 3 items). Such psychometric information, considered alongside relevant practical costs, can help her identify an efficient and psychometrically-sound measurement strategy for the large-scale study.

Generalizability and universes

From a G-Theory perspective, the key psychometric issue is the degree to which observed scores are generalizable. Researchers use measures based upon only a limited number of observations. For example, our hypothetical researcher's single-facet measurement strategy includes only three raters, and her multiple-facet strategy included only three raters and only three items. Such limitations raise concerns about the degree to which her scores represent anything psychologically general about the participants—anything beyond, for example, the potentially-idiosyncratic perceptions of her three raters. Thus, G-Theory conceptualizes measurement quality as the degree to which scores based on a limited number of observations per participant represent scores based on an infinite number of observations per participant.

That is, measurement quality is defined as the degree of generalizability *from* scores obtained through a measurement strategy based upon limited numbers of observations *to* scores that could (theoretically) be obtained from an unlimited set, or "universe," of observations. Imagine that a participant's behavior is observed and rated by every rater who could conceivably do so; that is, imagine that his behavior is rated by the entire "universe" of raters. Furthermore, imagine that all of these ratings are aggregated together. This theoretical aggregated score is the participant's "universe score," as computed for the rater facet.

From this perspective, the researcher's three raters are a sample from the universe of potential raters who could observe and rate participants' pro-social behavior. At least in theory, other raters might provide substantially-different ratings of the participants. The researcher should therefore be concerned about the degree to which the specific raters in her study represent the many other raters who could provide behavioral ratings. She hopes that her three raters produce scores representative of, generalizable to, or consistent with scores that would be obtained if a huge set of people had observed and rated participants' pro-social behavior. More specifically, the researcher hopes that variability in her participants' actual scores is consistent with variability in their "universe" scores (i.e., scores that would be obtained if the entire universe of potential raters had provided behavioral ratings).

Variance components

G-Theory allows researchers to estimate variance components, reflecting the variability of universe scores. For example, when evaluating her single-facet measurement design, the hypothetical researcher estimates a variance component reflecting the differences among scores that would be provided by the entire universe of potential raters. In a G-Theory analysis, researchers estimate a variance component for each facet of their measurement strategy, along with several additional components as discussed later.

Estimated variance components reflect the degree to which each facet of a measurement strategy affects scores. If a measurement facet has a relatively large variance component, then that facet has a relatively powerful effect on (i.e., creates variability in) scores produced by the measurement strategy. For example, if our researcher obtains a relatively large estimate for the "rater" facet, then she concludes that different raters would likely produce substantially-different ratings of pro-social behavior (even when rating the same participants).

Moreover, variance components have implications for the quality of a measurement strategy. For example, our researcher might consider using only three raters, and her data might produce a relatively large estimated variance component for the rater facet. Again, a large variance component would indicate that raters differ substantially in their ratings of pro-social behavior, and this might create concern about relying on only three raters. That is, because raters differ so substantially, a small number of raters might produce ratings with weak generalizability—their ratings might be dramatically different from those produced by a different set of raters. This is clearly a psychometric problem (i.e., which set of raters should be trusted, if either?), motivating the researcher to employ more raters, thereby obtaining scores with greater generalizability.

In sum, G-Theory relies on several fundamental concepts, including facets, generalizability, universe scores, and variance components. Next, these concepts are illustrated through a small, hypothetical data set reflecting a two-facet measurement strategy.

Conducting and Interpreting G-Theory Analysis

Through an illustrative G-Theory analysis, this section begins to reveal potential benefits of G-Theory as a psychometric tool. The example reflects a two-facet measurement strategy, in which three raters observe and rate the behavior of several participants by using three items ostensibly reflecting pro-social behavior.

Imagine that the hypothetical researcher collected the data in Table 9.1a as a small-scale pilot study intended to inform a measurement plan for a large-scale project. For this pilot study, each rater rates each of five participants on each item, using 7-point scales. The researcher plans to calculate a composite pro-social behavior score for each participant by averaging across all nine ratings. From a G-Theory perspective, the researcher hopes that observed differences among participants' composite scores are generalizable to the composite scores that would be obtained if participants were rated by the entire universe potential raters using the entire universe of pro-social behavior items. That is, the researcher hopes to be able to generalize across two measurement "universes." First, she hopes that the scores produced by the three raters are generalizable to scores that would be produced by an extremely large set of raters, and second, she hopes that the scores obtained via the three specific items are generalizable to scores that would be obtained if an extremely large set of items were used. Her analytic process begins by articulating the factorial structure of the measurement strategy.

Articulating the factorial structure

G-Theory analysis begins with examination of factors affecting the observed ratings, which in turn affect the psychometric quality of the composite scores. Typically, researchers use Analysis of Variance (ANOVA, or another variance

Table 9.1 Example data for two-facet G-Theory analysis

a Raw data

Partic.	Chris			Keith			Rachel		
	Conc.	Comp.	Supp.	Conc.	Comp.	Supp.	Conc.	Comp.	Supp.
Rufus	3	3	2	2	2	2	3	3	4
Xavier	2	1	2	2	3	1	4	4	5
Janet	3	2	3	3	3	2	3	2	2
Lolly	2	2	2	4	6	4	4	5	3
Bill	5	6	4	6	7	5	7	7	7

b Main effects

Partic.	Mean	Rater	Mean	Item	Mean
Rufus	2.67	Chris	2.80	Conc.	3.53
Xavier	2.67	Keith	3.47	Comp.	3.73
Janet	2.56	Rachel	4.20	Supp.	3.20
Lolly	3.56				
Bill	6.00				

c Interactions

	Part. × Rater				Part. × Item				Rater × Item		
	Chris	Keith	Rachel		Conc.	Comp.	Supp.		Conc.	Comp.	Supp.
Rufus	2.67	2.00	3.33	Rufus	2.67	2.67	2.67	Chris	3.00	2.80	2.60
Xavier	1.67	2.00	4.33	Xavier	2.67	2.67	2.67	Keith	3.40	4.20	2.80
Janet	2.67	2.67	2.33	Janet	3.00	2.33	2.33	Rachel	4.20	4.20	4.20
Lolly	2.00	4.67	4.00	Lolly	3.33	4.33	3.00				
Bill	5.00	6.00	7.00	Bill	6.00	6.67	5.33				

decomposition procedure such as "VARCOMP" in SPSS or "Proc Varcomp" in SAS) to decompose measurement data into relevant effects, subsequently using those results to estimate variance components for each effect. Thus, our hypothetical researcher uses ANOVA to explore variability across all 45 ratings (i.e., the ratings of the five participants on three items as rated by three raters), with results presented in Table 9.2. For this two-facet design, seven factors potentially affect variability in the ratings, paralleling the factors obtained from an ANOVA with three independent variables. Note that these analyses are "random effects," which will be discussed in more depth later.

The first, and focal, factor is the degree to which participants elicit differing ratings of pro-social behavior, as averaged across all raters and all items. Table 9.1b shows, for example, that Janet has the lowest average rating of pro-social

Table 9.2   ANOVA and generalizability results for example data

Effect	DF	SS	MS	$\hat{\sigma}^2$	% Var
Participant	4	76.80	19.20	1.86	.56
Rater	2	14.71	7.36	.31	.09
Item	2	2.18	1.09	.01	.00
Participant x Rater	8	18.40	2.30	.65	.19
Participant x Item	8	4.27	.53	.06	.02
Rater x Item	4	3.16	.79	.09	.03
Residual	16	5.73	.36	.36	.11
Total	44	125.25		3.34	1.000

behavior (2.56), as averaged across all raters and all items. In contrast, Bill has the highest average rating (6.00). For many applications of G-Theory, such variability among participants—the degree to which participants exhibit differing levels of the phenomenon being measured—is the "signal" that researchers wish to detect. Measurement is easiest, and measurement quality is often best, when participants differ substantially from each other—when there is a robust signal to be detected.

The second factor is the degree to which raters provide differing ratings, as averaged across all participants and all items—the degree to which some raters tend to see people as generally more or less pro-social than do other raters. As shown in Table 9.1b, the raters' average ratings range from 2.8 to 5.2. This suggests that, for example, Chris generally views participants as less pro-social than does Rachel.

The third factor is the extent to which items elicit differing ratings, as averaged across all participants and all raters. For example, the item main effects in Table 9.1b show minimal differences among the items, and the item means range only from 3.20 to 3.73. Thus, no item was dramatically "easier" or "harder" than the others, in terms of eliciting substantially higher or lower ratings.

The fourth, fifth, and sixth factors potentially driving variability in the ratings are two-way interactions. The *Participant by Rater interaction* reflects, roughly speaking, the degree to which raters provide different rank-orderings of the participants. The "Participant X Rater" values in Table 9.1c illustrate this, showing that the three raters are somewhat inconsistent with each other in their judgments of, for example, the difference between Rufus and Xavier. Chris sees Rufus as more pro-social than Xavier, but Keith sees no difference between the two, and Rachel sees Rufus as *less* pro-social than Xavier. Thus, the raters are somewhat inconsistent with each other, in terms of their ability to detect clearly the differences among participants' pro-social behavior (i.e., the differences between participants are somewhat inconsistent across raters). The *Participant by Item interaction* reflects the degree to which participants are rank-ordered differently across items. The "Participant X Item" values in Table 9.1c illustrate this to a small degree, showing that the differences among participants are only slightly inconsistent across items. For example, Rufus was rated lower than Janet in terms of "Expressing Concern," but he was rated as *higher* than Janet in terms of "Exhibiting Compassion" and "Offering Support." Thus, the items seem to be operating somewhat inconsistently with each other, in terms of their ability to reflect differences among participants' pro-social behavior. Overall, however, the "Participant X Item" interaction seems minimal in these data, suggesting that the rank order of participants is generally quite consistent from one item to another. Sixth, the *Rater by Item interaction* reflects the degree to which raters differ in their rank-orderings of the items, averaged across targets. The "Rater X Item" values in Table 9.1c illustrate this, again to a small degree, showing that the rank order of items is only slightly inconsistent across raters. For example, Chris rated the average participant as Expressing Concern to a greater degree than Exhibiting Compassion, but Keith rated the average participant as Expressing Concern to a *lesser* degree than Exhibiting Compassion. However, the "Participant X Item" interaction again seems minimal—the differences among items are generally quite consistent across raters.

The seventh and final factor affecting ratings in this strategy is the residual, capturing two elements in the current design. Because each rater provided a single rating of each participant on each item, the potential three-way interaction between participants, raters, and items cannot be separated from pure "error" variance. Thus, the residual term represents all variability in ratings that is unsystematic, inconsistent, or unrelated to the six factors that affect ratings systematically.

Differing factorial structures   The current two-facet design includes seven separable effects, but measurement strategies differ in their factorial structure in several ways. First, they differ in the *number of facets* affecting variability in the data. Simple measurement strategies include only a single facet. For example, a typical self-report strategy might require a sample of participants to complete a multi-item self-report measure of a single construct. In such cases, the sole measurement facet is the items, and the factorial structure includes a "main effect of participants," a "main effect of items," and a residual term. More complex designs include more extensive factorial structures that potentially include several main effects and interactions. In theory, there is no limit to the number of facets in a measurement design.

A second way in which factorial structures might differ is in terms of *random and fixed facets*. In G-Theory analysis, each facet is conceptualized as either random or fixed (though most applications treat facets as random). A random facet is one in which the facets' units that are used in the study are seen as a random sample from the universe of possible units; that is, they are seen as being exchangeable for other units from the same universe. For example, our hypothetical researcher may view the three raters in her study as being exchangeable for any other raters— she is not intrinsically interested in those specific raters, rather she sees them as being randomly selected from a universe of potential raters. Similarly, she might view the items as being exchangeable for other items that could be used to assess pro-social behavior. In contrast, measurement designs might include fixed facets, which arise when a researcher does not generalize beyond the specific units included in the analysis, or when all units of a facet are included in the study. For G-Theory, researchers consider the random/fixed issue for each facet. Thus, multiple-facet designs might include one or more random facets and one or more fixed facets. A full discussion of this distinction is beyond the scope of this chapter, but it has implications for a design's factorial structure (see also Nezlek, this set).

Finally, factorial structures differ in terms of *crossed versus nested facets.* In multiple-facet designs, pairs of facets are either crossed or nested. If data are collected for each combination of two facets, then the facets are considered crossed. The current two-facet example reflects crossed facets, in that each of the three raters rates each of the three items. In contrast, if each possible combination of two facets is not included in the design, then the facets are nested. For example, our researcher could ask raters to use different items—Chris might use two items ("Concern" and "Compassion"), Keith might use two different items, and Rachel might use yet another pair. In this design, each observer rates only two items, and Items are nested in Raters. This issue affects a design's factorial structure by determining the effects to be estimated. For example, the current design's "fully-crossed" structure allows seven effects to be estimated; however, if Items were nested in Raters, then only five effects could be estimated. Again, a full discussion is beyond the scope of this presentation, but such differences affect subsequent statistical estimations and the conclusions drawn from the analyses.

Computing variance components

After researchers understand a measurement design's factorial structure, conduct an ANOVA, and obtain Mean Squares values, they estimate a variance component for each effect. Table 9.2 presents the estimates ($\hat{\sigma}^2$ values) for the hypothetical data set, and Table 9.3 presents equations for calculating these values in this design. For example, the estimated variance component for the participant effect is:

$$\hat{\sigma}_p^2 = \frac{MS_p - MS_{pr} - MS_{pi} + MS_{Res}}{n_r n_i}$$

$$\hat{\sigma}_p^2 = \frac{19.200 - 2.300 - .533 + .358}{3 \times 3}$$

$$\hat{\sigma}_p^2 = \frac{16.725}{9}$$

$$\hat{\sigma}_p^2 = 1.858$$

Table 9.3   Equations for estimating variance components in the Participant x Rater x Item model

Effect	Equation
Participant	$\hat{\sigma}_p^2 = \dfrac{MS_p - MS_{pr} - MS_{pi} + MS_{Res}}{n_r n_i}$
Rater	$\hat{\sigma}_r^2 = \dfrac{MS_r - MS_{pr} - MS_{ri} + MS_{Res}}{n_p n_i}$
Item	$\hat{\sigma}_r^2 = \dfrac{MS_i - MS_{pi} - MS_{ri} + MS_{Res}}{n_p n_r}$
Participant x Rater	$\hat{\sigma}_{pr}^2 = \dfrac{MS_{pr} - MS_{Res}}{n_i}$
Participant x Item	$\hat{\sigma}_{pi}^2 = \dfrac{MS_{pi} - MS_{Res}}{n_r}$
Rater x Item	$\hat{\sigma}_{ri}^2 = \dfrac{MS_{ri} - MS_{Res}}{n_p}$
Residual	$\hat{\sigma}_{Res}^2 = MS_{Res}$

Notes: $\hat{\sigma}^2$ = estimated variance component, MS = Mean Square from ANOVA, n = number of units for the relevant facet.

In these equations (Table 9.3), MS refers to Mean Squares values obtained via ANOVA (e.g., MS_{pr} refers to the Mean Squares for the Participant X Rater interaction), and n refers to the number of units within each facet (e.g., n_r refers to the number of raters in the study).

The estimated variance components reveal the degree to which each facet affects ratings of pro-social behavior. Because a variance component is affected by both the magnitude of the facet's effect and the scale of measurement (e.g., a 7-point scale), the absolute size of a variance component is difficult to interpret. Therefore, variance components are usually most informative when compared to each other, for example, as proportions of total variability. Table 9.2 presents these proportions, computed as an effect's variance component divided by the sum of all variance components. For example, the participant effect accounts for nearly 60 percent of the variability in the current data set:

$$\frac{1.858}{1.858+.308+.008+.647+.058+.086+.358}=.559$$

The relatively large size of the "Participant effect" variance component suggests that there is a relatively strong signal to be detected by a researcher wishing to measure differences in participants' pro-social behavior. That is, it indicates that participants exhibited robust differences in their pro-social behavior.

Estimated variance components will always be based upon MS values and the numbers of units, but the precise equations depend on the design's factorial structure. That is, equations appropriate for this example's two-facet, fully random, fully-crossed design differ from those appropriate for a two-facet design that is mixed in terms of random/fixed or crossed/nested facets. The current design is perhaps prototypical, but details about alternative designs are available in other sources. In addition, statistical software such as SPSS and SAS will compute appropriate variance components if researchers specify the correct design.

Estimating generalizability

After researchers estimate variance components for the effects, they can evaluate the psychometric quality of their design through estimates of generalizability. By calculating generalizability coefficients, researchers estimate the degree to which scores from their study likely generalize across one or more universes of the measurement design. For example, our hypothetical researcher would likely calculate a generalizability coefficient to estimate the degree to which participants' scores (based upon three raters using three items) generalize across a universe of raters and across a universe of items.

Like traditional reliability (Chapter 4), generalizability coefficients reflect the clarity of a signal. When measuring psychological or behavioral differences among participants, researchers are essentially attempting to detect a signal (e.g., differences among participants) that is partially obscured by noise (e.g., random measurement error and other facets of the measurement strategy). Thus, a generalizability coefficient can be seen as:

$$\text{generalizability coefficient} = \frac{\text{Signal}}{\text{Signal} + \text{Noise}}$$

In the current hypothetical study, as with many studies, the "signal" is the differences among participants. The strength of this signal is captured by the relative size of the "Participant effect" variance component, reflecting the degree to which participants have differing scores as averaged across all other factors in the model (see Participant Main effects in Table 9.1b).

"Noise" includes factors that potentially mask this signal. The way in which noise is conceptualized depends upon researchers' measurement goals. Most measurement applications in social/personality psychology focus on detecting the relative standings of participants on the psychological construct being measured. For example, our hypothetical researcher wishes to detect accurately which participants exhibited a relatively high level of pro-social behavior and which exhibited relatively low levels; that is, she wants to quantify, as clearly as possible, the relative differences among the participants' levels of pro-social behavior. For such cases, researchers compute "relative" generalizability coefficients.[2]

For the current hypothetical measurement design and goal, noise includes three factors. The first is the *Participant × Rater interaction*, reflecting the degree to which participants were rank-ordered differently by the raters. As discussed earlier, the relevant values in Table 9.1c reveal that raters are somewhat inconsistent in their judgments of the differences between participants. Because the measurement goal is to obtain a generalizable measure of participants' differences in pro-social behavior, the Participant × Rater effect is noise because it indicates that the differences among participants is *not* consistent or generalizable across raters (to some degree). The second factor contributing noise is the *Participant × Item interaction*, reflecting the degree to which participants were rank-ordered differently across items. A large Participant × Item interaction would indicate that the differences among participants are inconsistent across items. A third source of noise is the *Residual*, reflecting all other unsystematic, inconsistent variability in ratings. By definition, unsystematic variability obscures any underlying rank-ordering of participants across observers and items, thus masking the signal.

The three remaining effects are *not* considered to be measurement noise because they would not obscure the rank-ordering of participants. As described earlier, the *Rater effect* reflects the degree to which some raters provide higher average ratings than others. Even if raters differ in their average ratings, this is unrelated to the consistency with which they rank-order the participants. That is, even though Chris generally rates participants as less pro-social than does Keith (i.e., there is some Rater effect), they consistently rate Rufus as less pro-social than Bill. Similarly, the *Item effect* reflects the degree to which some items elicit higher average ratings than others, but this is unrelated to the degree to which the items operate consistently in terms of the relative ordering of participants. Finally, the *Rater × Item interaction* reflects the degree to which raters provide different rank-orderings of items, as averaged across targets; however, this again is unrelated to the consistency with which raters or items rank-order participants.

After identifying the effects reflecting signal and noise for a given measurement design and goal, researchers can estimate a generalizability coefficient ($\hat{\rho}_p^2$). Using relevant variance components, researchers use an equation paralleling the conceptual signal/noise ratio to estimate the coefficient of generalizability for the participant effect:

$$\hat{\rho}_p^2 = \frac{\hat{\sigma}_p^2}{\hat{\sigma}_p^2 + \dfrac{\hat{\sigma}_{pr}^2}{n_r} + \dfrac{\hat{\sigma}_{pi}^2}{n_i} + \dfrac{\hat{\sigma}_{Res}^2}{n_r n_i}}$$

(Equation 9.1)

Note that the numerator of this equation includes the variance component for the participant effect, representing the signal to be detected. The denominator includes this signal, plus the three variance components representing noise. Further, the noise components are weighted by their respective number of units (i.e., the number of raters and the number of items)—larger numbers of units reduce the noise component in the denominator, which increases the generalizability coefficient.

To illustrate this computation, our hypothetical researcher uses the variance components presented in Table 9.2:

$$\hat{\rho}_p^2 = \frac{1.858}{1.858 + \dfrac{.647}{3} + \dfrac{.058}{3} + \dfrac{.358}{3 \times 3}}$$

$$\hat{\rho}_p^2 = \frac{1.858}{1.858 + .275}$$

$$\hat{\rho}_p^2 = .871$$

Interpreted on a 0–1 metric analogous to traditional reliability values, this coefficient suggests that the 3-rater/3-item measurement strategy produces scores that appear to be highly generalizable and thus psychometrically sound.

Equation 9.1 underscores a core difference between G-Theory and CTT, as discussed earlier. In CTT, measurement error is undifferentiated—observed scores are determined only by "True score" and a single "Error" component. Thus, CTT treats the nine ratings simply as nine ratings, not accounting for the factorial structure that includes systematic effects of rater differences, item differences, and the relevant interactions. In contrast, G-Theory allows researchers to differentiate, and thus understand, the systematic effects that different facets can have on measurement quality. This contrast, and the benefit provided by G-Theory, may be clearest when evaluating alternative measurement strategies.

Evaluating alternative measurement strategies

G-Theory's differentiation of measurement noise allows researchers to evaluate various measurement strategies, providing valuable information for planning efficient and effective research. Our hypothetical researcher might find, for example, that relatively few raters, but many items, are necessary. Alternatively, she might find that many raters, but few items, are needed. Such information, considered alongside practical costs, can maximize the efficiency and quality of her large-scale measurement strategy. In sum, the researcher's three-rater/three-item strategy has good generalizability ($\hat{\rho}_p^2 = .87$, as estimated earlier), but she can use G-Theory to potentially identify an even stronger or more efficient strategy. This is known as a "D-Study" because it informs decisions about future measurement strategies.

To conduct these analyses, the hypothetical researcher uses information from her pilot-study. By using the estimated variance components, she can evaluate the likely psychometric quality of measurement designs with varying numbers of raters and items. She enters these variance components into Equation 9.1, along with n values representing the potential number of raters and items she wishes to consider. For example, she estimates the relative generalizability for a measurement strategy that includes a single rater and two items:

$$\hat{\rho}_p^2 = \frac{1.858}{1.858 + \dfrac{.647}{1} + \dfrac{.058}{2} + \dfrac{.358}{1 \times 2}}$$

$$\hat{\rho}_p^2 = \frac{1.858}{1.858 + .855}$$

$$\hat{\rho}_p^2 = .685$$

This value might be too low, so she evaluates additional designs until she finds one having strong psychometric quality while, at the same time, being relatively cost-effective.

Table 9.4 and Figure 9.1 present estimated generalizability coefficients for several potential measurement strategies, based upon the pilot-study data. These values reveal several insights. First, as expected, greater numbers of raters and items produce better psychometric quality. Second, these benefits have diminishing returns. For example, the psychometric superiority of three raters over one rater is greater than the superiority of five raters over three raters. Third and most concretely, these values reveal the specific designs that could be acceptable or unacceptable for the researcher. For example, the values reveal that a generalizability of .81 could be achieved with only two raters using only two items. Depending on the costs (e.g., in time, effort, and/or money) associated with using additional raters and additional items, the researcher might decide that this level of generalizability is acceptable and that the measurement strategy is relatively cost-effective.

Summary

This chapter outlined basic concepts and logic of G-Theory, which can be seen as an ANOVA-based expansion of CTT. G-Theory is a flexible and powerful psychometric perspective in at least two important ways. First, it expands the conceptualization of reliability to account for the possibility that multiple facets can

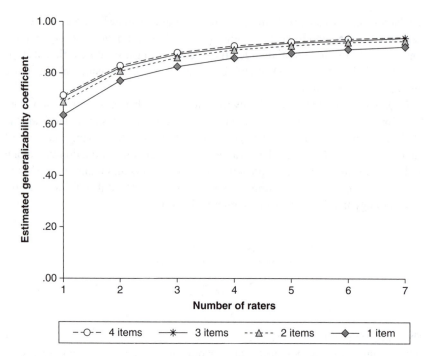

Figure 9.1   Relative generalizability coefficients as determined by numbers of raters and items

Table 9.4   Generalizability coefficients estimated using variance components

Raters (n_r)	1	2	3	4	5	1	2	3	4	5
Items (n_r)	1	1	1	1	1	2	2	2	2	5
Relative generalizability coefficient $(\hat{\rho}_p^2)$	.64	.77	.83	.86	.88	.68	.81	.86	.89	.91
Raters (n_r)	1	2	3	4	5	1	2	3	4	5
Items (n_r)	3	3	3	3	3	4	4	4	4	4
Relative generalizability coefficient $(\hat{\rho}_p^2)$	.70	.82	.87	.90	.91	.71	.83	.88	.90	.92

systematically affect the quality of a measurement strategy. Second, it provides statistical tools for evaluating the effects of each facet of a measurement design and for planning measurement designs that maximize quality and efficiency. There are many variations on the basic analysis presented in this chapter, in terms of factorial structure (e.g., differing numbers of facets, nested designs) and the measurement goals. Indeed, this flexibility is an appealing and powerful characteristic of G-Theory.

Notes

1 A CTT-based alternative to the "nine-item" approach would be to treat the strategy as two single-facet analyses. That is, the researcher could average across the three items for each rater, and apply CTT to the averaged rater scores; or she could average across the three raters for each item and apply CTT to those averaged item scores. Yet another alternative would be to examine the raters' responses for each item; for example, computing an alpha value (based on the three raters) for each of the three items. However, all of these approaches fail to differentiate effectively between the facets, or fail to do so in a way that reveals potentially important measurement information.

2 In some measurement contexts, test administrators might wish to use measurements in more absolute ways. For example, people enlisting in the United States Army take the Armed Services Vocational Aptitude Battery (ASVAB), and must score at least a 31 to be eligible (http://www.goarmy.com/learn/asvab.jsp, n.d. retrieved 6/10/2009). Thus, the Army is interested in a recruit's absolute score—whether it is higher than 31. For this measurement application, the Army is less concerned, if at all, with the relative scores among recruits. The difference between "relative" and "absolute" uses of test scores affects the way that "noise" is conceived in G-Theory. Because social/personality research focusses primarily on relative applications of measurement, the current discussion focusses only on relative uses. Discussion of absolute uses and their implications for G-Theory can be found elsewhere (Brennan, 2001; Furr & Bacharach, 2008).

10

Item Response Theory

This chapter introduces Item Response Theory (IRT), another important psychometric departure from Classical Test Theory (CTT). Although IRT's roots go back more than 50 years, it has enjoyed increased attention and development in social/personality psychology since the 1980s. This chapter introduces IRT's basic concepts, its differences from CTT, and its use in constructing and evaluating psychological scales. Interested readers can find additional details elsewhere (Hambleton et al., 1991; Van der Linden & Hambleton, 1997; Embretson & Reise, 2000).

IRT provides information about the quality of a scale's items and of the entire scale. Indeed, many applications of IRT begin with analysis of items. As discussed in this chapter, researchers often present graphical displays of items' psychometric parameters to reflect the items' properties. Such displays include Item Characteristic Curves (ICCs) and Item Information Curves (IICs), and they convey item-level information about psychometric quality. Item-level analyses are often followed by scale-level psychometric analyses. By combining information across item-level properties, researchers often present Test Information Curves (TICs) to reflect the overall psychometric quality of the scale itself. In addition, IRT can be extended to the examination of group differences in item functioning, to the identification of people who provide item response patterns that are unusual and potentially problematic, and to the application of computerized adaptive testing. As will be discussed, IRT has important qualities differentiating it from CTT. Most applications of IRT are conducted via specialized statistical software such as PARSCALE, BILOG, and MUTLTILOG, which are becoming quite user-friendly and manageable.

Factors Affecting Item Responses

According to IRT, a person's response to an item is affected by a quality of the person and by one or more qualities of the item. IRT arises from statistical models reflecting the probability that a given person will respond in a certain way to a given item. Perhaps more accurately, the models reflect the probability that a person having a given level of a psychological characteristic will respond in a certain way to an item having a given set of psychometric qualities. These probabilities are plotted in the ICCs often found in IRT analysis.

Respondent's level of the relevant psychological characteristic

The first factor affecting a person's responses to scale items is his or her standing on the psychological characteristic being assessed by those items. For example, when a person completes the Stress Reaction subscale of the Multidimensional Personality Questionnaire (MPQ; Tellegen, 1982), his or her responses are presumably affected by his or her level of reactivity to stress—a high level of reactivity increases the probability that he or she will endorse items referring to high levels of worry, difficulty sleeping, nervousness, startle, and irritation, and a low level decreases the probability.

Relatedly, most IRT applications are based upon the assumption that there is a single strong latent variable affecting responses to all items on a scale, and researchers typically use factor analysis to evaluate this assumption prior to conducting IRT analysis. There is no clear criterion or standard for evaluating this assumption, so researchers examine one or more pieces of information. For example, Smith and Reise (1998) conducted an IRT analysis of the MPQ's 23-item Stress Reaction subscale. They found that a single factor accounted for 39 percent of the variance in the scale and that the ratio of first-to-second eigenvalues was above 9. They thus concluded that the scale was sufficiently unidimensional to proceed with the IRT analysis. Other researchers have proceeded on the basis of first-to-second eigenvalue ratios of 3:1 or 4:1, and some additionally examine the magnitude of factor loadings from a one-dimensional structure as guidelines (e.g., do all items load at least .30 on the factor?). Still others use Confirmatory Factor Analysis to evaluate a unidimensional model prior to conducting an IRT analysis.

In IRT, the level of the relevant underlying psychological characteristic is conceptualized in terms of standard scores and is labeled theta (θ). Thus, a person with an average level of the underlying psychological characteristic has $\theta = 0$, a person who is one standard deviation below the mean on the characteristic has $\theta = -1$, and so on.

Item difficulty

An item's difficulty is another factor affecting a person's response to the item. The notion of difficulty is perhaps clearest in the assessment of abilities or knowledge. For example, some potential items on a mathematics test (e.g., "If $x = 5$, then $x^2(x^3 - 3) =$_____") are more difficult to answer correctly than are other items (e.g., "If $x = 5$, then $x + 2 =$_____"). That is, some items require a higher level of ability or knowledge than do other items. Although difficulty might be clearest in terms of abilities or knowledge, it also applied to assessments of constructs such as attitudes or traits. Consider two potential items on a scale assessing Stress Reaction: 1) "I have felt stressed at least once in my life;" and 2) "Even in mildly-stressful situations, I lose all emotional control." In terms of a tendency toward reactivity, the second item is a more extreme statement than the first item—only someone who has an extremely high level of reactivity would truthfully endorse the second item, whereas someone with a moderate or even low amount of reactivity would likely endorse the first. In this sense, the second item is the more difficult item—a higher level of the construct is required to produce a genuine endorsement of that item.

As this example implies, item difficulty can be framed in terms of theta (i.e., in terms of levels of the underlying psychological characteristic). Indeed, IRT quantifies item difficulty as the theta value associated with a .50 probability of responding in a specific way to an item. For example, the second (i.e,, relatively difficult) stress reaction item above might have a difficulty level of, say, 2.7, indicating that someone with a level of stress reaction 2.7 standard deviations above the mean has a 50/50 chance of endorsing the item (recall that theta values are expressed as standardized scores). Similarly, the first item might have a difficulty level of, say, −.2, indicating that someone with a level of stress reaction .2 standard deviations below the mean has a 50/50 chance of agreeing to the item. These values suggest that a higher level of stress reaction is required in order to have even a 50/50 chance of endorsing the second item.

Dichotomous items In the simplest case of scales having items with only two response options, each item has a single difficulty level. That is, dichotomous items allow only two possible responses (e.g., correct/incorrect, true/false, yes/no, agree/disagree), and IRT produces one difficulty parameter estimate for each item. For example, each true/false item on the MPQ's Stress Reaction subscale describes a tendency to experience negative emotional states such as anxiety, guilt, and irritability. In their IRT analysis of this scale, Smith and Reise (1998) reported a difficulty value for each item, computed separately for males and females (see the "Difficulty" columns in their Table 3). For example, analysis of males' responses revealed a difficulty of −.33 for item 1 on the scale and a difficulty of 1.09 for item 6. This indicates that item 1 was "easier" than was item 6—specifically, a relatively low level of stress reaction (i.e., a level of stress reaction about one-third of a standard deviation below the mean) is required for a male to have a .50 probability of responding "true" to item 1, but a much higher level of stress reaction (i.e., a level more than one standard deviation above the mean) is required for a male to have a .50 probability of responding "true" to item 6.

Polytomous items In social/personality psychology, many scales—perhaps most—include items with more than two response options. Social/personality psychologists frequently use "Likert-type" items allowing multiple response possibilities, often having 5-point or 7-point response formats (e.g., disagree, neutral, agree, etc.). IRT analysis of such items is an extension of analysis of dichotomous items.

In IRT, each polytomous item has multiple difficulty values. Specifically, an item with m response options will have $m-1$ difficulty values, with the response options being conceptualized as $m-1$ dichotomies. For example, consider Oishi's (2006) IRT analyses of the 5-item Satisfaction With Life Scale (SWLS; Diener et al., 1985). Participants responded to items using a 7-point response format ranging from 1 (strongly disagree) to 7 (strongly agree). Thus, analyses produced six difficulty values for each item. For polytomous items, each difficulty value reflects the level of the psychological construct at which respondents have a .50 probability of moving from one response option to another. Oishi's analysis of Chinese respondents revealed, for example, that item 1 on the SWLS had the following difficulty parameters: 1) −2.68, 2) −.87, 3) −.35, 4), −.10, 5) 1.08, and 6) 2.89 (see the "b" values in Oishi's Table 3). The first value indicates that a person with even a substantially low level of life satisfaction (i.e., more than two and a half standard deviations below the mean) has a 50/50 chance of responding higher than "strongly disagree" to item 1. Similarly, the second difficulty value indicates that a person with a somewhat higher level of life satisfaction—though still relatively low at .87 standard deviations below the mean—has a 50/50 chance of responding higher than "disagree" to item 1. More generally, the values show that an increasing level of life satisfaction is required to make higher and higher levels of agreement to item 1. Overall, Oishi's analysis produced six difficulty values for each SWLS item, revealing a similar pattern for each.

Item discrimination

Along with difficulty, item discrimination is a property potentially affecting participants' responses to items on psychological scales. An item's discrimination is the degree to which the item differentiates people with low levels of the underlying construct from people with high levels. In a sense, it reflects the degree to which the item reflects the underlying psychological construct; in this way, it is conceptually similar to an item-total correlation or an item's factor loading (Chapter 4). Discrimination values usually range from zero to 3.0 or more, with large values reflecting better psychometric quality. In a typical IRT analysis, each item has a single discrimination value. This is true for both dichotomous and polytomous items.

For example, Smith and Reise's (1998) analysis of the MPQ Stress Reaction scale produced a discrimination value for each item. Among males, these values ranged from a low of .43 (for item 18, with content regarding "getting over humiliation easily") to a high of 1.46 (for item 13, with content regarding "being nervous often"). Although such specifics were not of primary interest to Smith and Reise, they indicate that item 18 may be poor—it may not clearly differentiate males who have a tendency for low stress reaction from those who have a tendency for high stress reaction. In contrast, item 13 (with the largest discrimination value) works relatively well.

Guessing

Though not examined frequently in social/personality applications of IRT, a third item property potentially affecting participants' responses to test items is chance or guessing. Thus an item's guessing value reflects the probability that a respondent will respond correctly to an item, based purely on chance or guessing. The lack of "correct" answers on most social/personality scales makes this parameter irrelevant in such applications of IRT.

Summary

According to IRT, several factors affect a person's responses to items on psychological measures. Along with the person's level of the psychological construct being assessed by an item, several item properties could potentially affect his or her responses—item difficulty, item discrimination, and a guessing parameter are three such properties that might affect responses. In most psychological applications of IRT, researchers gauge the psychometric properties of items and, ultimately, of scales. Thus, social/personality psychologists using IRT are primarily interested in obtaining and reporting item difficulty and item discrimination, with direct implications for the psychometric quality of items and scales. The current section reviewed factors potentially affecting responses to items on psychological scales. These effects are articulated precisely through measurement models, which are described briefly in the next section, with emphasis on one that is relatively simple but relevant for many social/personality applications of IRT.

IRT Measurement Models and Response Probabilities

As a general psychometric approach, IRT encompasses many specific measurement models reflecting the factors potentially affecting individuals' responses to items on a psychological scale or test. All IRT models are framed in terms of the probability that a respondent with a specific level of the relevant underlying construct will respond in a specific way to an item with a specific set of psychometric properties. Furthermore, they reflect nonlinear associations between the probability of responding in a certain way to an item and theta (i.e., the level of the relevant psychological construct).

IRT models differ in at least two ways. First, they differ in the number of item parameters affecting individuals' responses. The simplest IRT measurement models include only item difficulty (along with individuals' levels of the relevant psychological construct). More complex IRT measurement models include two or more item parameters, such as item discrimination and guessing. A second way in which IRT models differ is in terms of the items' number of response options. The simplest models are appropriate for items having only two response options—for example, correct/incorrect, true/false, yes/no, and agree/disagree (i.e., dichotomous items). More complex models are used for items having three or more response options—for example disagree, neutral, agree (i.e., polytomous items).

For example, the two-parameter logistic model (2PL) is an IRT model for scales having dichotomous items (e.g., the true/false items on the MPQ Stress Reaction scale), and its parameters are item difficulty and item discrimination. According to the 2PL, the probability that a person will respond in a specific way to an item (e.g., "true" or 1, versus "false" or 0) can be modeled as:

$$P\left(X_{is} = 1 \middle| \theta_s, \beta_i, \alpha_i\right) = \frac{e^{\left(\alpha_i\left(\theta_s - \beta_i\right)\right)}}{1 + e^{\left(\alpha_i\left(\theta_s - \beta_i\right)\right)}} \qquad \text{(Equation 10.1)}$$

In this model, X_{is} refers to response (X) made by subject s to item i, θ_s refers to subject s's level of the relevant psychological construct, β_i refers to the difficulty of item i, α_i refers to the discrimination of item i, $X_{is} = 1$ refers to a "true" response (or a correct response, an agreement, etc.), and e is the base of the natural logarithm (i.e., 2.7182818 …). Thus, $P(X_{is} = 1 | \theta_s, \beta_i, \alpha_i$ indicates that the probability (P) that subject s will respond "true" to item i is conditional upon the subject's level of the underlying construct (θ_s), the item's difficulty (β_i), and the item's discrimination (α_i).

Consider item 13 from Smith and Reise's (1998) analysis of the MPQ Stress Reaction scale. The use of the 2PL to model males' responses suggested that this item had a difficulty value of $\beta_{13} = .99$ and a discrimination value of $\alpha_{13} = 1.46$. Thus, a male with an average level of Stress Reactivity $(\theta = 0)$ would have a low probability $(P = .19)$ of responding "true" to item 13:

$$P = \frac{e^{\left(1.46(0-.99)\right)}}{1 + e^{\left(1.46(0-.99)\right)}} = \frac{e^{(-1.45)}}{1 + e^{(-1.45)}} = \frac{.23}{1 + .23} = .19$$

In contrast, a male with a high level of Stress Reactivity (say, a level 1.5 standard deviations above the mean) would have a higher probability $(P = .68)$ of responding "true" to the item:

$$P = \frac{e^{\left(1.46(1.5-.99)\right)}}{1 + e^{\left(1.46(1.5-.99)\right)}} = \frac{e^{(.74)}}{1 + e^{(.74)}} = \frac{2.10}{1 + 2.10} = .68$$

There are at least two points to note about these responses probabilities. First is the intuitively reasonable finding that the respondent with the lower level of stress reaction has a lower likelihood of genuinely responding "true" to the item. Second, the less-reactive respondent's probability of responding "true" is less than .50, and the more-reactive respondent's probability is greater than .50. This difference underscores the logic of item difficulty as the theta level (i.e., the level of the relevant psychological construct) at which a respondent has a 50/50 chance of responding "true" to the item. As reported by Smith and Reise and as reflected in the calculations above, item 13's difficulty level is .99 for males, meaning that a male respondent needs to have a level of stress reaction that is (essentially) one standard deviation above the mean in order to have a .50 probability of responding "true" to item 13. Because the first respondent's Stress Reactivity ($\theta = 0$) was lower than the item's difficulty ($b_{13} = .99$), his probability of responding "true" is below .50. In contrast, the second respondent's Stress Reactivity ($\theta = 1.5$) was greater than the item's difficulty, and therefore his probability of responding "true" to the item is above .50.

Another comparison underscores the logic of item discrimination. Consider the two hypothetical participants' response probabilities for item 15 on the MPQ Stress Reaction scale. According to Smith and Reise (1998), this item's difficulty is $b_{15} = .94$ and its discrimination is $a_{15} = .95$. Thus, item 15 is similar to item 13 in terms of difficulty (i.e., $b_{13} = .99$, $b_{15} = .94$), but it is less discriminating (i.e., $a_{13} = 1.46$, $a_{15} = .95$). Entering the two hypothetical respondents' theta levels into the 2PL model along with the item parameters for item 15, we find that the average-Reactive respondent ($\theta = 0$) has a .29 probability of responding "true" to the item and the high-Reactive respondent ($\theta = 1.5$) has a .63 probability of responding "true." Note that the .34 difference between these probabilities (.63 − .29 = .34) is less than the .49 difference between the participants' response probabilities for item 13 (.68 − .19 = .49). The relatively small difference in response probabilities for item 15 reflects the fact that its discrimination parameter is lower than the one for item 13. Thus, item 15 is poorer at differentiating between respondents having differing levels of stress reaction.

The 2PL is applicable to many psychological scales with dichotomous items, but other measurement models are used for items having three or more response options. Perhaps the most frequently-used such model in social/personality psychology is the Graded Response Model (GRM), which is applicable for polytomous items. For the GRM, each item comprises several response probabilities, one for each response option. For example, Oishi's (2006) analysis of the 7-point Likert-type items on SWLS scale was based upon the GRM. As mentioned earlier, this analysis revealed the following difficulty parameters for item 1: 1) −2.68, 2) −.87, 3) −.35, 4), −.10, 5) 1.08, and 6) 2.89 (along with a discrimination parameter of 1.53). Based upon these values and Equation 10.1, a respondent with an average level of SWL would have the following response probabilities for this item (there would actually be six response probabilities).

Probability of endorsing a response option higher than "Strongly Disagree" (the first response option):

$$P = \frac{e^{\left(1.53(0-(-2.68))\right)}}{1+e^{\left(1.53(0-(-2.68))\right)}} = \frac{e^{(4.10)}}{1+e^{(4.10)}} = \frac{60.364}{1+60.364} = .984$$

Probability of endorsing a response option higher than "Disagree" (the second response option):

$$P = \frac{e^{\left(1.53(0-(-.87))\right)}}{1+e^{\left(1.53(0-(-.87))\right)}} = \frac{e^{(1.33)}}{1+e^{(1.33)}} = \frac{3.785}{1+3.785} = .791$$

Probability of endorsing a response option higher than "Slightly Agree" (the fourth response option):

$$P = \frac{e^{\left(1.53(0-(-.10))\right)}}{1+e^{\left(1.53(0-(-.10))\right)}} = \frac{e^{(.153)}}{1+e^{(.153)}} = \frac{1.165}{1+1.165} = .538$$

Thus, these values suggest that a respondent with an average level of Satisfaction with Life would be extremely likely (98 percent chance) to endorse a response option greater than "Strongly Disagree," very likely (79 percent chance) to endorse an option greater than "Disagree," somewhat likely (54 percent chance) to endorse an option greater than "Slightly Agree," and so on. Again, when applied to a respondent's level of the underlying construct, the GRM produces probabilities reflecting the likelihood that the respondent would respond "higher than" each response option (except for the highest response option, of course).

In most applications of IRT, researchers are more interested in response probabilities across a wide range of construct levels than in only one or two specific probabilities. Thus, they often examine and present item characteristic curves (ICCs) or item response functions for each item on a scale. As illustrated next, ICCs display the probabilities with which people of various construct levels will answer an item in a certain way.

Plotting Response Probabilities: Item Characteristic Curves

In many applications of IRT, researchers present graphical displays of items' properties in the form of ICCs. Figure 10.1 presents an ICC for three items from the MPQ Stress Reaction scale, based upon information from Smith and Reise's (1998) application of the 2PL model. Along the X-axis, ICCs plot a range of construct levels; along the Y-axis they plot response probabilities ranging from 0 to 1.0. In plotting response probabilities derived from the 2PL, an ICC can be plotted for each item on a scale, revealing the likelihood that an individual with any particular construct level will endorse each item.

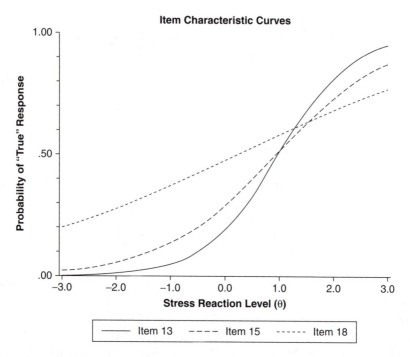

Figure 10.1   Three Item Characteristic Curves

Consider the ICCs in Figure 10.1 and note the probability that a person with an average level of stress reaction will answer the "true" to item 13. The point on item 13's ICC that is directly above the "0" point on the X-axis (recall again that the construct level is in standardized units) lies close to .20 on the Y-axis. Indeed, calculations presented earlier revealed that a person with average Stress Reactivity has a .19 probability of responding "true" to this item. The other items' ICCs reveal that a person with average Stress Reactivity has about a .30 probability of answering "true to item 15 and little less than a .50 probability of answering "true" to item 18. Thus, ICCs reflect the likelihoods that respondents of any trait levels would answer "true" to any item.

There are two points to note about ICCs such as those in Figure 10.1. First, an item's difficulty is apparent in the X-axis point at which its ICC intersects the .50 point on the Y-axis. This reflects the fact that an item's difficulty is the construct level at which a respondent has a 50/50 chance of responding "true" to the item (or answering it correctly, or agreeing to it, etc.). For example, Figure 10.1 shows that item 13's ICC intersects the .50 point on the Y-axis at approximately $\theta = 1.0$ on the X-axis. This intersection location is determined by the item's difficulty— recall that $b_{13} = .99$.

Second, an item's discrimination is apparent in the slope of its ICC. Items discriminating well among respondents at different construct levels have a sharply-sloped ICC, and items discriminating poorly have a flatter ICC. These differences are apparent in Figure 10.1, showing that item 13 has the sharpest slope ($a_{13} =$ 1.46), item 15 has a somewhat less sharp slope ($a_{15} = .95$) and item 18 has the flattest slope ($a_{18} = .43$). The sharpness of an ICC's slope underscores the meaning of discrimination, in that a sharply-sloped ICC shows the probability of responding "true" to an item changing dramatically within a narrow range of construct levels. For example, item 13's ICC increases dramatically within a range of 1.5 standard deviations of Stress Reaction levels (i.e., from approximately $\theta = 0$ to $\theta = 1.5$). That is, an average respondent has a dramatically lower chance of responding "true" to item 13 than does a respondent with a Stress Reaction level that is 1.5 standard deviations above average. Therefore, if a person responds "true" to item 13, we can be quite confident that he or she truly has a higher level of Stress Reaction than someone who answers "false." In contrast, item 18's ICC increases very gradually across a wide range of Stress Reaction levels. Thus, a respondent with a very low level of Stress Reaction has only a somewhat lower chance of responding "true" to item 18 than does a respondent with a very high level. The fact that a respondent responds "true" to item 18 does not provide clear information about his or her level of Stress Reaction—even though he responds "true" to item 18, we cannot be highly confident that he actually has a higher level of Stress Reaction that someone who responds "false."

Again, the 2PL is but one measurement model, and ICCs based upon other models may appear somewhat different. For example, when applied to polytomous items, the GRM produces more complex ICCs that include multiple curves for each item—one curve for each response option. In such analysis, each of an item's curves represents the probability that people of various construct levels are likely to choose a specific response option (e.g., the likelihood that people of varying construct levels will respond "strongly agree" to an item). Figure 10.2 presents ICC curve(s) based upon the parameter estimates for SWLS item 1, as reported by Oishi (2006). Consider for example, the curve for the "Strongly Disagree" option. This curve suggests that, someone who has an extremely low level of SWL (say, $\Theta = -3$) has relatively high likelihood of choosing this response option, but that people with higher levels of SWL are less likely to choose this response option. Indeed, respondents who are "only" average on SWL have less than a 5 percent likelihood of "Strongly Disagreeing" with item 1. Consider, in contrast, the "Slightly Agree" option. This curve suggests that, someone who is slightly above average in SWL (say, $\Theta = .5$) has relatively high likelihood of choosing this response option, but that people with lower or higher levels of SWL are less likely to choose this response option. Another way of viewing this ICC is to consider the likely response choices for a respondent who has any given level of SWL. For example, a respondent who is very high on SWL

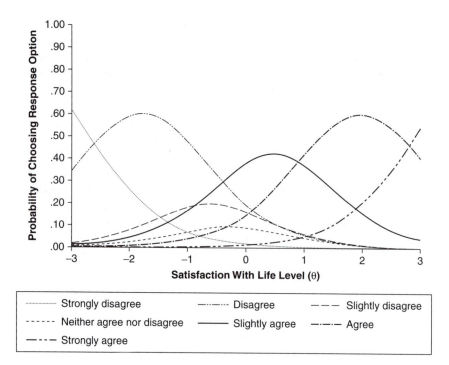

Figure 10.2 Item Characteristic Curves for a polytomous item with seven response categories

(say, $\Theta = 2$) is most highly likely to "Agree" with item 1, somewhat less likely to "Slightly Agree" or "Strongly Agree," and very unlikely to choose any other response option. Thus, ICCs for polytomous items provide detailed information about the likely response choices across a range of construct levels.

In sum, researchers often examine and present ICCs in order to illustrate basic item characteristics such as difficulty and discrimination. These characteristics guide researchers who develop and evaluate psychological scales, for example, by revealing items that might be eliminated from the scale (i.e., those with low discrimination values). However, IRT-based psychometric evaluation goes beyond these qualities, providing important insights into "item information" and "test information," discussed in the following section.

Item Information and Test Information

In most psychological research, a scale's purpose is to differentiate (i.e., discriminate) people with relatively high levels of a psychological construct from people with lower levels. An item provides useful information when differences in participants' response to the item accurately reflects differences in their construct levels. By extension, a scale provides good information when differences in participants' scale scores accurately reflect differences in their construct levels.

The IRT-based concepts of "item information" and "test information" parallel the CTT concept of reliability. Recall that CTT conceptualizes a single reliability for scale responses, reflecting the degree to which observed scores are correlated with true scores on the attribute being measured. In contrast, IRT suggests that a set of scale responses does not have a single "reliability." Rather, a scale might provide psychometrically-stronger information for some people than for others— that is, a scale (and each item within the scale) might provide better information at some construct levels than at others.

Item information

The notion that an item's quality or a scale's quality can vary across construct levels might seem odd, but consider again two items potentially used to assess Stress Reaction: 1) "I have felt stressed at least once in my life;" and 2) "Even in mildly-stressful situations, I lose all emotional control." The first item seems relatively "easy" in that many people would respond "true" to it. Indeed, only the most non-reactive people would likely respond "false" to this item. Thus, this item likely differentiates extremely non-reactive people from everyone else, but it does not discriminate among everyone else. That is, it does not differentiate among respondents with moderate or high levels of stress reaction (i.e., people with moderate, high, or very high levels of stress reaction would all likely respond "true" to the first item). In contrast, the second item seems to be more "difficult" in that few people would respond "true" to it. Presumably, only the most intensely reactive people would endorse this item, and people with only moderate or low reactivity would respond "false" to the item. Thus, the second item likely differentiates extremely reactive people from everyone else, but it does not discriminate among everyone else. That is, it does not differentiate among people with moderate or low levels of reactivity. In sum, the first item provides good information about extremely low levels of stress reaction, and the second item provides good information about extremely high levels of stress reaction.

From an IRT perspective, scales should include items with information covering the entire range of construct levels along which researchers would like to differentiate. For example, a scale that includes only items like the first item would be useful for differentiating among people with low levels of stress reaction but not for differentiating among people with moderate or high levels. Somewhat better would be a scale that included both the first and second items; however, such a scale would provide little or no information among people with somewhat low, moderate, and somewhat high levels of stress reaction. Thus, a researcher who wishes to create a scale differentiating across the entire range of stress reaction would need to include items that might differentiate among people with more moderate levels of the construct (e.g., "I often get upset when I feel stressed").

IRT can be used to estimate the amount of information that an item provides across a wide range of construct levels. For example, according to the 2PL, the amount of information provided by an item for a given level of the psychological construct is (Reise, 1999):

$$I_i(\theta) = \alpha_i^2 P_i(\theta)(1 - P_i(\theta))$$
(Equation 10.2)

In this equation, α_i^2 is the item's (squared) discrimination value, and $P_i(\theta)$ is the item's response probability associated with the given construct level (see Equation 10.1, above). For example, according to Smith and Reise's analysis of the MPQ Stress Reaction scale (1998), item 13 provides the following levels of information at three different construct levels (recall that item 13's discrimination is $a_{13} = 1.46$, and note that the $P_i(\theta)$ values are computed separately via Equation 10.1):

$$I_{13}(\theta = -1.5) = (1.46)^2(.03)(1 - .03) = .06$$

$$I_{13}(\theta = 0) = (1.46)^2(.19)(1 - .19) = .33$$

$$I_{13}(\theta = 1.5) = (1.46)^2(.68)(1 - .68) = .46$$

With higher values reflecting greater amounts of information (i.e., better psychometric quality), these values reveal that item 13 provides more information about respondents with levels of stress reaction that are about 1.5 standard deviations above the mean, somewhat less information about respondents with average levels of stress reaction, and almost no information about respondents with levels of stress reaction that are well below the mean.

Researchers (or software packages) can compute and plot information values for a wide range of construct levels to produce Item Information Curves (IICs), such as those presented in Figure 10.3a. For scale development and evaluation, IICs reflect the psychometric value of each item on a scale.

IICs reveal at least two insights. First, they reveal construct levels at which each item is most informative. For example, Figure 10.3a indicates that item 13 provides good discriminative information among participants with above-average levels of Stress Reaction, particularly among participants who are approximately one standard deviation above average in reactivity. In fact, items are maximally informative at construct levels corresponding to their difficulties (recall that $b_{13} = .99$).

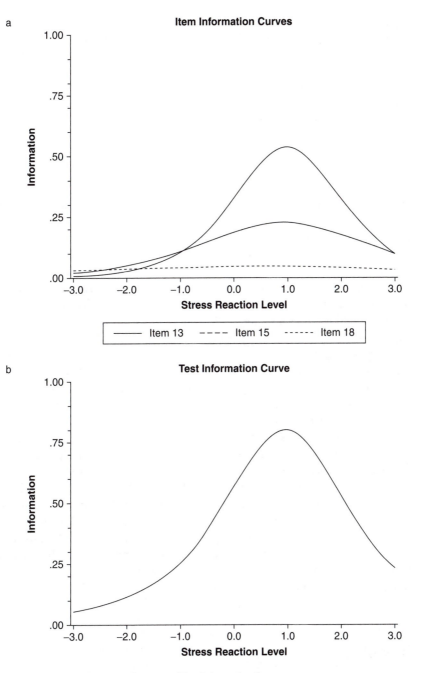

Figure 10.3   Item Information Curves and Test Information Curve

The second insight revealed in an IIC is the amount of information provided by the item. For example, compare the amount of information conveyed by items 13 and 15, as reflected in the heights of their IICs. The IICs imply that, even though both items are maximally informative at approximately the same construct levels, item 15 provides *more* information than does item 13 (i.e., better discrimination among respondents). Furthermore, both items are clearly more informative than item 18, which provides almost no discriminative information across the entire range of Stress Reaction.

Test information

Of course, when researchers use psychological scales, they must understand the quality of the scale as a whole. Therefore, item information values can be combined to produce test information values. For any given construct level, item information values can be summed to produce a test information value at that construct level. Temporarily treating the three items in Figure 10.3a as an entire test, Figure 10.3b is a Test Information Curve (TIC) presenting test information values for the "three-item Stress Reaction scale" across a wide range of construct levels (of course, the actual test information values for the Stress Reaction scale would reflect 23 items on the full test). For example, the test information provided at a construct level of $\theta = 1.5$ is the sum of the three items' information values at $\theta = 1.5$ (i.e., $.72 = .47 + .21 + .04$, with item information values computed via Equation 10.2).

As illustrated in this TIC, test information values can be computed across a range of construct levels. Overall, these values reflect the construct levels at which the scale is most and least informative. For example, the "three-item" Stress Reaction scale is most useful for differentiating among respondents at relatively high levels of Stress Reaction. Specifically, the highest test information values are found at approximately $\theta = 1.5$, with the lowest below $\theta = 0$. Thus, although this three-item version is relatively informative for highly Reactive respondents, it is not very useful for differentiating among respondents who are below average on Reactivity. With this in mind, we might consider expanding this "three-item" version of the scale to include items informative at relatively low construct levels.

The logic and process of item and test information applies to other IRT models (beyond the 2PL) as well. A full discussion/illustration is beyond the scope of this chapter, but producers of IRT analysis can generally conceptualize item and test information as outlined in this section.

Uses of IRT

IRT has been applied in many psychological domains, such as the measurement of abilities, attitudes, traits, and many other social/personality phenomena. In these domains, there are several important uses of IRT.

One key use of IRT is the construction, evaluation, and improvement of psychological scales. With information about item and test properties (e.g., ICCs, item information, test information), scale-developers can identify items reflecting an appropriate range of construct levels and having good discriminative ability. Guided by IRT analyses, researchers can generate scales with strong psychometric properties across a range of construct levels. For example, Fraley et al. (2000) used IRT to evaluate several attachment scales, providing useful recommendations about the modification and use of one scale in particular.

A second key use of IRT is examination of differential item function (DIF). DIF occurs when an item functions differently in different groups of respondents. That is, it occurs when an item's properties in one group differ from its properties in another group, and it indicates that groups cannot be meaningfully compared on the item (see Chapter 6's discussion of Test Bias). For example, Smith and Reise (1998) examined DIF for males and females on the Stress Reaction scale MPQ, finding that items related to "emotional vulnerability and sensitivity in situations that involve self-evaluation" were easier for females to endorse, but that items related to "the general experience of nervous tensions, unexplainable moodiness, irritation, frustration, and being on-edge" were easier for males. These results suggest that measures of negative emotionality will show larger gender differences when "female DIF type items" are overrepresented but will show small gender differences when "male DIF type items" are overrepresented. Such insights can inform development and interpretation of important psychological measures and can enhance understanding of psychological constructs themselves.

A third potential use of IRT is examination of "person-fit"—the possibility that some respondents may respond in a way that does not "fit" a reasonable pattern of responses to the items. Consider again two potential Stress Reaction items: 1) "I have felt stressed at least once in my life;" and 2) "Even in mildly-stressful situations, I lose all emotional control." A person who agrees with the second item should also agree with the first item—that is, a person who easily loses all emotional control would also genuinely admit to feeling stressed at least once in his or her life. However, we would not necessarily expect the reverse—the fact that someone has felt stressed at least once does not imply that he or she easily loses emotional control. Indeed, we would be quite surprised to find someone who disagrees with item 1 but agrees with item 2. Thus, there are four possible response patterns for these items, three of which have straightforward interpretations:

Pattern	Item 1–Item 2	Interpretation
1	Disagree–Disagree	Non-reactive
2	Agree–Disagree	Somewhat reactive
3	Agree–Agree	Very reactive
4	Disagree–Agree	Unclear

Analysis of person-fit identifies people whose response pattern does not fit the expected patterns of responses to a set of items. Poor (i.e., unusual) person-fit has several possible implications such as cheating, low motivation, cultural bias of the test, intentional misrepresentation, or even problems in scoring or administration. Furthermore, in social/personality psychology, poor person-fit could indicate that a person's personality (or attitudinal structure, or whatever is being assessed) is unusual in that it produces responses that do not fit the "typically-expected" pattern of responses (Reise & Waller, 1993).

A fourth use of IRT is in facilitating Computerized Adaptive Testing (CAT)—computerized test administration intended to produce accurate and efficient assessments of individuals' psychological characteristics. CAT is based upon large pools of items, all of which are intended to assess a given psychological characteristic and all of which have been evaluated via IRT. When a person begins the test, the CAT system presents items of average difficulty. The system then adapts the test to fit respondent's construct level. For example, if a person begins with several correct answers or endorsements, then the system presents items at above-average difficulty levels. However, if a person starts with incorrect answers or non-endorsements, then the system presents items at below-average difficulty levels. As the system adaptively matches items to respondents' response patterns and construct levels, two respondents might end up taking tests comprising of different items. Although it might seem counterintuitive that two people's test scores are comparable if they have responded to different items, the purpose of CAT is to present items that target each person's construct level efficiently. That is, it presents only those items relevant to precise estimation of each examinee's construct level. For people who clearly have a high level of the measured construct, nothing is gained by having them respond to very easy items. Similarly, for people who clearly have a lower level of the construct, nothing is gained by requiring them to respond to difficult items. Therefore, instead of presenting a single long test to every respondent, a CAT system presents each respondent with only as many items as are useful for pinpointing his or her construct level.

Summary

In sum, IRT is a psychometric framework encompassing a variety of statistical models that represent connections among item responses, examinee construct levels, and item characteristics. A deep understanding of characteristics such as item difficulty and item discrimination can guide development, interpretation, and improvement of psychological scales.

References

American Educational Research Association, American Psychological Association, and National Council on Measurement in Education (1999). *Standards for Educational and Psychological Testing*. Washington, DC: American Educational Research Association.

Armor, D.J. (1974). Theta reliability and factor scaling. In H.L. Costner (ed.), *Sociological Methodology*. San Francisco: Jossey-Bass.

Baer, R.A. & Miller, J. (2002). Underreporting of psychopathology on the MMPI-2: A metaanalytic review. *Psychological Assessment*, 14, 16–26.

Brennan, R.L. (2001). *Generalizability Theory*. New York: Springer-Verlag.

Borsboom, D., Mellenbergh, G.J., & Van Heerden, J. (2004). The concept of validity. *Psychological Review*, 111, 1061–1071.

Brown, T.A. (2006). *Confirmatory Factor Analysis for Applied Research*. New York: Guilford.

Burisch, M. (1984). Approaches to personality inventory construction: A comparison of merits. *American Psychologist*, 39, 214–227.

Byrne, B. (2001). *Structural Equation Modeling with AMOS: Basic Concepts, Applications, and Programming*. Mahwah, NJ: Lawrence Erlbaum Associates.

Byrne, B. (2006). *Structural Equation Modeling with EQS* (2nd edn). Mahwah, NJ: Erlbaum.

Campbell, D.T. & Fiske, D.W. (1959). Convergent and discriminant validation by the multitrait-multimethod matrix. *Psychological Bulletin*, 56, 81–105.

Cohen, B.H. (2001). *Explaining Psychological Statistics* (2nd edn). New York: Wiley.

Cohen, J. (1990). Things I have learned (so far). *American Psychologist*, 45, 1304–1312.

Cohen, J. & Cohen, P. (1983). *Applied Multiple Regression/Correlation Analysis for the Behavioral Sciences* (2nd edn). Hillsdale, NJ: Erlbaum.

College Board. (n.d.). SAT Reasoning Test. Retrieved from http://www.collegeboard.com/student/testing/sat/about/SATI.html

Costello, A. & Osborne, J. (2005). Best practices in exploratory factor analysis: Four recommendations for getting the most from your analysis. *Practical Assessment, Research & Evaluation*, 10, 1–9.

Couch, A. & Keniston, K. (1960). Yea-sayers and nay-sayers: Agreeing response set as a personality variable. *Journal of Abnormal and Social Psychology*, 20, 151–174.

Cronbach, L.J., Gleser, G.C., Nanda, H., & Rajaratnam, N. (1972). *The Dependability of Behavioral Measurements: Theory of Generalizability for Scores and Profiles*. NY: Wiley.

Crowne, D.P. & Marlowe, D. (1960). A new scale of social desirability independent of psychopathology. *Journal of Consulting Psychology*, 24, 349–354.

Diamantopoulos, A. & Siguaw, J.A. (2000). *Introducing LISREL: A Guide for the Uninitiated*. London: Sage.

Diener, E., Emmons, R.A., Larsen, R.J., & Griffin, S. (1985). The Satisfaction with Life Scale. *Journal of Personality Assessment*, 49, 71–75.

Dunn, D.S. (2009). *Research Methods for Social Psychology*. Malden, MA: Wiley-Blackwell.

Edwards, J.R. (1995). Alternatives to difference scores as dependent variables in the study of congruence in organizational research. *Organizational Behavior and Human Decision Processes*, 64, 307–324.

Embretson, S.E. (1983). *Construct Validity: Construct Representation versus Nomothetic Span. Psychological Bulletin*, 93, 179–197.

Embretson, S.E. & Reise, S. (2000). *Item Response Theory for Psychologists*. Mahwah, NJ: Erlbaum.

Fabrigar, L.R., Krosnick, J.A., & MacDougall, B.L. (2006). Attitude measurement: Techniques for measuring the unobservable. In M.C. Green, S. Shavitt, & T.C. Brock (eds.), *Persuasion: Psychological Insights and Perspectives*. Thousand Oaks, CA: Sage.

Fabrigar, L.R., Wegener, D.T., MacCallum, R.C., & Strahan, E.J. (1999). Evaluating the use of exploratory factor analysis in psychological research. *Psychological Methods*, 4, 272–299.

Feldt, L.S. & Brennan, R.L. (1989). Reliability. In R.L. Linn (ed.), *Educational Measurement* (3rd edn). Washington, DC: American Council on Education; Macmillan.

Floyd, F.J. & Widaman, K.F. (1995). Factor analysis in the development and refinement of clinical assessment instruments. *Psychological Assessment*, 7, 286–299.

Fraley, R.C., Waller, N.G., & Brennan, K.A. (2000). An item-response theory analysis of self-report measures of adult attachment. *Journal of Personality and Social Psychology*, 78, 350–365.

Funder, D.C. & Ozer, D.J. (1983). Behavior as a function of the situation. *Journal of Personality and Social Psychology*, 44, 107–112.

Furr, R.M. (2009). Personality psychology as a truly behavioural science. *European Journal of Personality*, 23, 369–401.

Furr, R.M. & Bacharach, V.R. (2008). *Psychometrics: An Introduction*. Thousand Oaks, CA: Sage.

Furr, R.M., Wagerman, S.A., & Funder, D.C. (2009). Personality as manifest in behavior: Direct behavioral observation using the revised Riverside Behavioral Q-sort (RBQ-3). In C.R. Agnew, D.E. Carlston, W.G. Graziano, & J.R. Kelly (eds.), *Then a Miracle Occurs: Focusing on Behavior in Social Psychological Theory and Research*. New York: Oxford University Press.

Gosling, S.D., Rentfrow, P.J., & Swann, W.B., Jr. (2003). A Very Brief Measure of the Big Five Personality Domains. *Journal of Research in Personality*, 37, 504–528.

Gosling, S.D., Vazire, S., Srivastava, S., & John, O.P. (2004). Should we trust Web-based studies? A comparative analysis of six preconceptions about Internet questionnaires. *American Psychologist*, 59, 93–104.

Greenleaf, E.A. (1992). Measuring extreme response style. *Public Opinion Quarterly*, 56, 328–351.

Hambleton, R.K., Swaminathan, H., & Rogers, H.J. (1991). *Fundamentals of Item Response Theory*. Newbury Park, CA: Sage.

Hatcher, L. (1994). *A Step-by-Step Approach to Using the SAS System for Factor Analysis and Structural Equation Modeling*. Cary, NC: SAS Institute.

Howell, D.C. (1997). *Statistical Methods for Psychology* (4th edn). Belmont, CA: Duxbury.

Hoyle, R.H. (2011). *Structural Equation Modelling for Social and Personality Psychology*. London: Sage.

Hu, L.T. & Bentler, P.M. (1999). Cut-off criteria for fit indexes in covariance structure analysis: Conventional criteria versus new alternatives. *Structural Equation Modeling*, 6, 1–55.

Jackson, D.N. (1971). The dynamics of structured personality tests: 1971. *Psychological Review*, 78, 229–248.

Jackson, D.L., Gillaspy, J.A., & Purc-Stephenson, R. (2009). Reporting practices in confirmatory factor analysis: An overview and some recommendations. *Psychological Methods*, 14, 6–23.

John, O.P. & Benet-Martinez, V. (2000). Measurement: Reliability, construct validation, and scale construction. In H.T. Reis & C.M. Judd (eds.), *Handbook of Research Methods in Social and Personality Psychology*. New York: Cambridge University Press.

John, O.P. & Srivastava, S. (1999). The Big Five Trait Taxonomy: History, measurement, and theoretical perspectives. In L.A. Pervin & O.P. John (eds.), *Handbook of Personality: Theory and Research* (2nd edn). New York: Guilford Press.

Kline, R.B. (1998). *Principles and Practice of Structural Equation Modeling*. New York: Guilford Press.

Knowles, E.S. & Nathan, K. (1997). Acquiescent responding in self-reports: Social concern or cognitive style. *Journal of Research in Personality*, 31, 293–301.

Kraemer, H.C., Periyakoil, V.S., & Noda, A. (2002). Kappa coefficients in medical research. *Statistics in Medicine*, 21, 2109–2129.

Krosnick, J.A., Judd, C.M., & Wittenbrink, B. (2005). Attitude measurement. In D. Albarracin, B.T. Johnson, & M.P. Zanna (eds.), *Handbook of Attitudes and Attitude Change*. Mahwah, NJ: Erlbaum.

Leach, C.W., van Zomeren, M., Zebel, S., Vliek, M., Pennekamp, S.F., Doosje, B., Ouwerkerk, J.P., & Spears, R. (2008). Group-level self-definition and self-investment: A hierarchical (multi-component) model of in-group identification. *Journal of Personality and Social Psychology*, 95, 144–165.

Lees-Haley, P.R. (1996). Alice in validityland, or the dangerous consequences of consequential validity. *American Psychologist*, 51, 981–983.

Maxwell, S.E. & Delaney, H.D. (2000). Designing experiments and analyzing data: A model comparison perspective. Mahwah, NJ: Erlbaum.

McArdle, J.J. (1996). Current directions in structural factor analysis. *Current Directions in Psychological Science*, 5, 10–17.

Messick, S. (1989). Validity. In R.L. Linn (ed.), *Educational Measurement* (3rd edn). New York: Macmillan.

Miller, M.B. (1995). Coefficient alpha: A basic introduction from the perspectives of classical test theory and structural equation modeling. *Structural Equation Modeling*, 2, 255–273.

Nezlek, J.B. (2011). *Multilevel Modeling for Social and Personality Psychology*. London: Sage.

Nunnally, J.C. & Bernstein, I.H. (1994). *Psychometric Theory* (3rd edn). New York: McGraw Hill.

O'Brien, E.J. & Epstein, S. (1988). *MSEI: Multidimensional Self-Esteem Inventory*. Odessa, FL: Psychological Assessment Resources.

Oishi, S. (2006). The concept of life satisfaction across cultures: An IRT analysis. *Journal of Research in Personality*, 41, 411–423.

O'Muircheartaigh, C., Krosnick, J.A., & Helic, A. (2000). Middle alternatives, acquiescence, and the quality of questionnaire data. Retrieved June 23, 2009 from http://harrisschool.uchicago.edu/About/publications/working-papers/pdf/wp_01_3.pdf

Ozer, D.J. (1985). Correlation and the coefficient of determination. *Psychological Bulletin*, 97, 307–315.

Paulhus, D.L. (1991). Measurement and control of response bias. In J.P. Robinson, P.R. Shaver, & L.S. Wrightsman (eds.), *Measures of Personality and Social Psychological Attitudes*. New York: Academic Press.

Paulhus, D.L. (2002). Socially desirable responding: The evolution of a construct. In H. Braun, D.N. Jackson, & D.E. Wiley (eds.), *The Role of Constructs in Psychological and Educational Measurement*. Hillsdale, NJ: Erlbaum.

Raykov, T. (2004). Behavioral Scale Reliability and Measurement Invariance Evaluation Using Latent Variable Modeling. *Behavior Therapy*, 35, 299–331.

Reise, S.P. (1999). Personality measurement issues viewed through the eyes of IRT. In S. Embretson & S. Hershberger (eds.), *The New Rules of Measurement: What Every Psychologist and Educator Should Know*. Mahwah, NJ: Erlbaum.

Reise, S.P. & Waller, N.G. (1993). Traitedness and the assessment of response pattern scalability. *Journal of Personality and Social Psychology*, 65, 143–151.

Robins, R.W., Hendin, H.M., & Trzesniewski, K.H. (2001). Measuring global self-esteem: Construct validation of a single-item measure and the Rosenburg Self-Esteem Scale. *Personality and Social Psychology Bulletin*, 27, 151–161.

Rogers, R. (2008). *Clinical Assessment of Malingering and Deception* (3rd edn). New York: Guilford Press.

Rosenthal, R. & Rubin, D.B. (1982). A simple, general purpose display of magnitude of experimental effect. *Journal of Educational Psychology*, 74, 166–169.

Shavelson, R.J. & Webb, N.M. (1991). *Generalizability Theory: A Primer*. Newbury Park, CA: Sage.

Shrout, P.E. & Fleiss, J.L. (1979). Intraclass correlations: Uses in assessing rater reliability. *Psychological Bulletin*, 2, 420–428.

Smith, L.L. & Reise, S.P. (1998). Gender differences on negative affectivity: An IRT study of differential item functioning on the multidimensional personality questionnaire stress reaction scale. *Journal of Personality and Social Psychology*, 75, 1350–1362.

Swami, V., Furnham, A., Chamorro-Premuzic, T., Akbar, K., Gordon, N., Harris, T., Finch, J., & Tovee, M.J. (in press). More than just skin deep? Personality information influences men's ratings of the attractiveness of women's body sizes. *Journal of Social Psychology*.

Tellegen, A. (1982). *Brief Manual of the Multidimensional Personality Questionnaire*. Unpublished manuscript, University of Minnesota.

Thompson, B. (2004). *Exploratory and Confirmatory Factor Analysis: Understanding Concepts and Applications*. Washington, DC: American Psychological Association.

Tucker, K.L., Ozer, D.J., Lyubomirsky, S., & Boehm, J.K. (2006). Testing for measurement invariance in the satisfaction with life scale: A comparison of Russians and North Americans. *Social Indicators Research*, 78, 341–360.

Van der Linden, W.J. & Hambleton, R.K. (eds.) (1997). *Handbook of Modern Item Response Theory*. New York: Springer.

Van Dierendonck, D. (2005). The construct validity of Ryff's scales of psychological wellbeing and its extension with spiritual wellbeing. *Personality and Individual Differences*, 36, 629–643.

Visser, P.S., Krosnick, J.A., & Lavrakas, P. (2000). Survey research. In H.T. Reis & C.M. Judd (eds.), *Handbook of Research Methods in Social Psychology*. New York: Cambridge University Press.

Watson, D., Clark, L.A., & Tellegen, A. (1988). Development and validation of brief measures of Positive and Negative Affect: The PANAS scales. *Journal of Personality and Social Psychology*, 54, 1063–1070.

Wegener, D.T. & Fabrigar, L.R. (2004). Constructing and evaluating quantitative measures for social psychological research: Conceptual challenges and methodological solutions. In C. Sansone, C.C.C. Morf & A.T. Panter (eds.), *The SAGE Handbook of Methods in Social Psychology*. New York: Sage.

Westen, D. & Rosenthal, R. (2003). Quantifying construct validity: Two simple measures. *Journal of Personality and Social Psychology*, 84, 608–618.

Whitley, B.E., Jr. (2002). *Principles of Research in Behavioral Science* (2nd edn). New York: McGraw-Hill.

Zumbo, B.D. (2007). Validity: Foundational issues and statistical methodology. In C.R. Rao and S. Sinharay (eds.), *Handbook of Statistics: Vol. 26. Psychometrics*. Elsevier Science B.V.: The Netherlands.

Index